Goodnight Mom, I love you

Goodnight Mom, I love you

Karen Ritter Kelly

Copyright © 2019 by Karen Ritter Kelly.

Library of Congress Control Number:		2018915272
ISBN:	Hardcover	978-1-9845-7468-8
	Softcover	978-1-9845-7467-1
	eBook	978-1-9845-7466-4

All rights reserved. No part of this book may be reproduced or transmitted in any form or by any means, electronic or mechanical, including photocopying, recording, or by any information storage and retrieval system, without permission in writing from the copyright owner.

The views expressed in this work are solely those of the author and do not necessarily reflect the views of the publisher, and the publisher hereby disclaims any responsibility for them.

Scripture quotations marked NIV are taken from the Holy Bible, New International Version®. NIV®. Copyright © 1973, 1978, 1984 by International Bible Society. Used by permission of Zondervan. All rights reserved. [Biblica]

Any people depicted in stock imagery provided by Getty Images are models, and such images are being used for illustrative purposes only.
Certain stock imagery © Getty Images.

Print information available on the last page.

Rev. date: 12/28/2018

To order additional copies of this book, contact:
Xlibris
1-888-795-4274
www.Xlibris.com
Orders@Xlibris.com
784560

CONTENTS

Prologue ix

Harvest Time 1

My Darkest Hour 9

Mavericks 23

Seize The Moment 34

Christmas 36

Hamburgers, Tacos, Or Pizza 39

Secrets Of The Heart 52

The Chicken Walk 61

Free-Fallen 66

Oakie Olympics 70

Graveyard Friends 74

Tapestry Of Our Life 86

Epilogue 89

I dedicate this book to
Buddy Kelly
Brandon Pruscha
Whitney Richards-Daniels

Prologue

More than a hundred people solemnly walked in unison, the glow of their candles flickering from the slight breeze that brought a chill to the night. The red and white flashing lights from fire engine no. 54 blended with the flashing lights of the ambulance as they slowly followed the procession of the candlelight vigil. The strobe-like effect of the lights, illuminating the darkness, brought attention to the family as the mourners approached their home. Coming out onto the porch, a young couple held one another and wept as their two-and-a-half-year-old daughter sought comfort in the arms of a family member. One by one, coworkers, friends, and friends of friends presented the couple with bouquets of flowers as the Reach Air Ambulance circled their home, a mark of respect, honoring their five-month-old son who died suddenly the day before.

    I could see that the parents were overwhelmed with the outpouring of love, and I could feel their pain. It is a pain that no words can describe. A pain so severe that it squeezes at your heart with such intensity it hurts to even breathe. I desperately wanted to go to the couple and tell them that someday the pain will lessen and, in time, the joy will return. I wanted to tell them that the morning will come when they will be able to celebrate their son's life. Instead, I stood in the distance and harbored my feelings in my heart because I knew better. I knew that the words I had to share were not the words they needed or wanted to hear. Their wounds were too raw. They needed to feel the pain so that the healing could begin.

Tanya, my neighbor, whispered that both parents were paramedics. She said they saved lives for a living and questioned why God allowed death to steal the life of their healthy baby boy. Shouldn't they be exempt? "I just don't understand," she softly cried. "They are the nicest people you'd ever want to meet. Why? Why do bad things have to happen to good people?"

I'm sorry, Tanya, no one is exempt from death. We are born to die. Some sooner than others.

Death also came to my family suddenly and stole one of my most precious treasures. Death's darkness came barging into my life like a roaring lion and sucked the joy right out of me. Along with the horrific pain of my seventeen-year-old son's death, I entered one of the greatest battles I would ever have to fight. The darkness of death threatened me daily, but I refused to let it devour me. I invite you to take a journey with me so that I can share how the amazing grace of God kept me breathing through my darkest hour and beyond.

*Let us not become weary in doing good,
For at the proper time we will reap a
harvest If we do not give up.*

—Galatians 6:9

Harvest Time

The fragrance of the cut grass lingered in the air, inviting me to remove my flip-flops. I wiggled my toes in its softness, allowing the coolness of each blade to gently massage my feet. I am reminded of the country girl that I truly am. My eyes roamed along the stretch of land, searching for dandelions and buttercups, but there weren't any. All I saw were rows and rows of multicolored flowers—some that will never wilt. A scrub jay fluttered from a nearby tree and landed in a puddle. He lowered his beak to take a drink from the pool of water then tilted his head back so that he could swallow.

As I closed my eyes and lifted my face to the spring sunshine, I felt the presence of my best friend. I asked, "How is it that I can stand here, surrounded by death, and still be able to see life and smell its sweet aroma?" Kneeling, I arranged daffodils in a brass vase. I lightly rubbed my fingertips along the name engraved on the memorial plaque and I asked, "How can I feel peace within my soul while in the midst of so much grief and sorrow?"

My friend embraced me and whispered, "Because you believe, Karen. You believe in a faith that is far beyond your comprehension. A faith that has grown from a seed as tiny as a mustard seed, and it has given you hope." A single tear rolled down my cheek as I remembered the day the seed was planted.

It was October 31, 1999, and I was sitting in the sanctuary of Harvest Time Assembly of God in Brentwood, California. My oldest son, Buddy, was sitting beside me.

Watching the congregation of young and old, I noticed that most were standing and singing with their hands lifted while others were clapping to the beat of the music. Some people were weeping. I'd like to say that I was also caught up in the passion, but truth was, I couldn't believe that I was amidst a church full of God-fearing Bible-reading holy rollers. My thought was, "Lord, what has Buddy dragged me into now?" I glanced at my son to see how he was reacting to the worship service and saw that his head was bowed. I had never seen him like that, and the pain on his sweet face reminded me of why I was there. I was looking for a miracle. A miracle to bring peace to my family.

A tragic accident that took the lives of two teenagers that my sons had grown up with led Buddy to Harvest Time Church, and two weeks later, I followed him. Buddy returned to the church after the funerals because his heart was broken. I returned, after the funerals, because of fear. I was afraid that one of my sons would be next.

The message that Pastor Dennis Reynolds conveyed captivated me. With compassion in his voice and tears in his eyes, he spoke of a man named Jesus that I only knew as the Son of God. He said He was the King of Kings, Lord of Lords, the Mighty Messiah. Pastor Reynolds said He was the Prince of Peace. The Prince of Peace—who was this man named Jesus?

Although I was desperate, I was not willing to step forward when the pastor called for salvation. Each time he extended the invitation, I was deaf to his cries. I was squirming in my seat when I felt the first nudge from my son. Turning to see what he wanted, I saw him nodding toward the altar. I shook my head no and turned away, only to feel him nudging me again. He continued to nudge me with his elbow, and when that no longer got my attention, he started tapping me with his foot. Each successive tap was firmer than the one before, aggravating me to a point where I wanted to scream. Looking straight ahead, with clutched teeth, I quietly growled, "Knock it off!"

"Mom," he whispered, "you need Jesus."

I could feel the tightness in my chest as I struggled to hold back my tears. I knew his words were true. With mixed emotions, I went to the altar because I knew that if I did not step forward, our battle would have escalated into a knockdown drag-out fight right there in the sanctuary.

As the pastor led me to the Lord, I was totally unprepared for the river of tears that poured down my cheeks. The pride and aggravation I carried to the altar was washed away as the grace of God descended upon me. I went home that Sunday with a massive headache, but the next morning, I woke up with a sense of peace none like I had ever known. That sense of peace continued throughout the remainder of 1999, and I rang in the New Year with a grateful heart.

During the winter of 2000, I faithfully attended church each Sunday. My heart was on fire, and there was a hunger deep within my soul. I yearned to learn the true Gospel of Jesus Christ and began to attend a Bible study on Wednesday evenings. As I grew, so did my faith, and I began to share what I was learning with my youngest son, Mikey. Although he had strong opinions, Mikey was open to discussions. I frequently invited him to church, but he always declined. I wasn't concerned about Mikey. He was a well-rounded sixteen-year-old that did well in school and was involved in leadership and sports. He made good choices, so I knew that someday, in God's time, he would give his heart to the Lord. On Easter Sunday, I gave both boys a teen study Bible. Mikey took his to his room and emerged later with a few comments. In the days that followed, I didn't know if he was still reading his Bible. I never asked him, but I did pray that he was. The confirmation came when he started asking questions. One of the most profound questions he asked was, "Mom, can you love Jesus if you don't know Him?"

"Some may think they love Him," I replied, "but I don't think you can fully feel the extent of that love until you have developed a relationship with Him."

"How do I do that?" he asked.

"Talk to Him, Mikey. Talk to Him like you are talking to your best friend," I said.

Our conversation continued until Mikey was satisfied and I knew by the look in his eyes and the expression on his face that he would reflect on what we discussed.

The year 2000 was a real challenge for me. I spent a lot of time at the altar asking for prayer. While Mikey was picking up his Bible, Buddy was putting his down. He was eighteen year old, and it frightened me because I remembered how I was that age. I always pray for him. I asked God to help him make good choices, to protect him, and to bring my son home safe every time he leaves.

I learned the importance of being a prayerful mother. I also realized that Christians are not exempt from trials and tribulations. In August, our family's hearts were broken when my mom suddenly passed away and six weeks later, on September 17, the same day I was baptized in water, my sister Betty passed away. Her four-year battle with multiple myeloma was finally over. No longer would she have to endure pain and suffering.

I welcomed 2001 with a hopeful heart. I didn't think I would ever have to endure another year like the one I had just gone through. I was teaching Sunday school and "making a joyful noise" singing in the choir. What a hoot because I could not carry a tune, and they let me sing anyway. I served with a cheerful heart and was faithful to my commitments. Surely, goodness would come my way.

In March, Freedom High School's leadership class was going on their annual Disneyland trip. Mikey had to be at the school at four o'clock in the morning. After checking in, we headed for the Oakland airport. Mikey was driving. He was a good driver so I felt comfortable and relaxed enough to slouch in the passenger seat. It was before the rush hour, and the traffic was light. Although it was still dark, the sky was clear and the view of dawn on the horizon gave promise of a beautiful springlike day.

I was about to doze off when Mikey announced, "I'm ready now."

In a monotone voice, I asked, "Ready for what?"

"You know," he said, "ready to accept Jesus into my heart."

Bolting straight up from my slouched position, I noticed that we were just beginning to enter the Caldecott Tunnel and asked, "Can it wait till we get through the tunnel?"

"It might be too late," he said.

"It's never too late," I replied.

In the wee quiet hours of a Monday morning, going southbound on Highway 13, I was given the honor to lead my precious son to the Lord. We drove the rest of the way to the airport in silence. Our huge grins were words enough. There was peace in our souls, and with the peace came two joyful hearts.

In the days that followed, it was a joy to watch Mikey's spiritual growth. One of his greatest challenges was forgiveness, and it was awesome to see him rekindle broken relationships.

My heart aches as I write the final pages of a chapter that I will complete, but will never truly close because of the shock of what would come in the fall of 2001.

September 11, the spilling of blood on US soil sent our nation into mourning. The fact that thousands were killed by acts of terrorism paralyzed millions as they watched New York City's World Trade Center crumble. Two beams from the structure had fallen, forming the shape of a cross. They were beams that were made of steel, but they reflected images more precious than gold. During all the death and destruction that evil had caused, God left his mark announcing that He was there. In our weakness, He was there to give us strength and goodness would prevail. To many, the image of the cross brought comfort as they grieved. I too was in awe of the cross. It was a big cross, and I was reminded of what it represented.

Talk of war and rumors of a possible draft upset our family, as I'm sure it upset many others. My husband, Bud, who served two tours in Vietnam, knew the ugliness of war. He did not want that for his sons, and the thought that they could be drafted saddened him immensely. Mikey was unusually quiet the day of the attacks, which surprised me. He was not one to hold his tongue. He had his opinions and had no problem letting his voice be heard, but 9/11 momentarily left him speechless. When he was finally able to sort out his feelings, he shared how he hated war but stated that if he were drafted, he would serve his country with pride, and if he died, then so be it; at least he would have died for a cause. With that, his mind was put to rest, and he embraced each day with a determination to live his life to its fullest.

Buddy, on the other hand, is the son who stores his emotions in a bottle and only releases some of his feelings when the pressure is building up. He is the son who would sit back and observe what was happening around him and quietly take it all in. He watches and waits, and if things get out of control, he pounces. After 9/11, he made a single statement that summed it all up. He said that he did not like war, but terrorism in America was unacceptable and he hoped that the United States would go after the terrorists. That is a nicer version of what he really said.

Add a few "four-letter" words, and the anger he felt would be apparent.

In my quiet moments, I prayed for our nation and refused to let the horrific events of 9/11 hold me captive. I had finally understood that God was in control, and I surrendered it all to Him. Several weeks later, I got a phone call that Buddy had been stabbed with a broken bottle. A helicopter had been called to airlift him to the nearby trauma center, but he refused to board. He insisted that his friends bring him home. Although I wasn't hysterical, I was very upset. How could a mother not be? I paced the house anxiously, waiting for him; and when Buddy finally arrived, I could see that he was in distress. I took one look at his back and knew he needed immediate medical attention. The wound was deep and ugly, so when he arrived at the trauma center, they took him right in—no waiting that night! What surprised me was the presence of so little blood. What surprised the doctor was how close the injury was to his spine and that he had no spinal damage. What amazed us both was the huge hunk of glass that was found embedded in Buddy's back compared to the tiny hole in his jersey that it had managed to tear through. The doctor removed the glass, stitched him up, and released him. My son was going to be fine: I was a mess. I believe that I witnessed a miracle that evening. Through the grace of God, Buddy was saved, his purpose in life not yet completed.

October was to bring a calmness that lasted well into November. Mikey was thriving, and Buddy was . . . well, let's just say Buddy was Buddy.

November 20, two days before Thanksgiving, I received a phone call at work that took my breath away and chilled every fiber of my being. In a broken voice, my husband gently told me that our son had been in a car accident and was airlifted to the trauma center. When I arrived at the emergency room, I was told that he was in critical condition and immediately called my church for prayers. Moments later, the doctor pronounced him dead. At one o'clock on a Tuesday afternoon, my precious son went to live with the Lord. My worst fear had happened, and I wanted to die too. I walked out of the hospital with nothing but a little Ziplock bag that contained my son's keys and wallet. They were covered with little slivers of glass. My heart was broken, but I clung to my faith because I knew that the only way I was going to survive this nightmare was to trust in God.

A gentle breeze brushed against my bare arms, indicating that sunset had arrived. My best friend embraced me once again and said, "It's time to go home, Karen. It's time for a new harvest. The crop is waiting."

"Yes, I know," I replied. I slowly walked to my car, and as I was about to get in, I looked over at my son's grave and I cried, "Abba Father, I miss my Mikey! This is such a big cross to bear."

"I know you miss your son, my child. And though the cross may seem big, always remember, I am here and will continue walking with you. When the cross gets too heavy, just call out my name and I will help carry the weight."

In my distress I called in to the Lord; I called out to my God.
From His temple He heard my voice;
My cry came to His ears.

—2 Samuel 22:7

My Darkest Hour

November 19, 2001, began like any other typical day in the Kelly household. Waking up to the five-thirty alarm screaming at me started my day with the usual Monday morning blues. I had planned to leave home early so that I could put in an extra hour of overtime at work. Instead, I slapped at the snooze button a couple of times, then got out of bed with the attitude of another day and another dollar. Then I remembered that I only had a two-day workweek. It was Thanksgiving week, and I had scheduled a vacation day on Wednesday so that I could have five glorious days off. Mikey, my youngest son, and I bought the ingredients for pumpkin pie and planned to make them Wednesday because he would also be on Thanksgiving break. I was excited! It had been a while since I had taken time off work for my own pleasure. Rushing around like a maniac looking for my car keys and, as usual, finding them in an off-the-wall place, I grabbed my purse, beat on Mikey's door, and hollered as I passed by his bedroom. "Mikey, it's seven o'clock. Time to get up. Have a good day. I love you!"

In a groggy voice, he replied, "Love you too."

I arrived at work, put in my eight hours, and came home. Everyone was tired, so I went to get fried chicken and side dishes to go with it. Mikey was my healthy eater and did not like fried chicken, so I bought him the makings for a hoagie. He had plans to go to his girlfriend Stephanie's house and did not want to waste any precious time making a hoagie, so he tolerated the fried chicken. I'll always remember what he said as he loaded his plate with mashed potatoes, gravy, coleslaw, a roll, and the smallest piece of chicken he could find: "This is like a Thanksgiving meal."

Mikey was a funny guy. He always managed to crack me up with laughter. He would say some of the goofiest things. How could he compare the greasy fried chicken to Thanksgiving dinner? I turned to look at him, intending to comment about his comment and busted up with laughter. When Mikey did not like what he was eating, he would not let the food touch his lips. I could not help but laugh because he looked so silly scraping the chicken off the fork with his teeth: his lips puckered like a fish. The joy that child gave me warmed my heart a thousand times over. He inhaled his food, practically swallowing the chicken whole, and headed out the door. That meal will be embedded in my mind forever because it was to be our last supper together.

A few minutes later, Buddy, my oldest son, came running in to tell me I needed to go listen to the truck. He said it would scare me. I went out to hear the whining sound of the engine as Mikey was trying to start the truck. I was about to offer him a ride when it finally turned over and purred like a cat. It sounded like the battery needed replacing, but I figured it would be okay for him to use it. I told Mikey to go ahead, use the truck, and to call if he had trouble starting it later. I did not give it a second thought, and as he left, I did not give him a time to be home.

Mikey was a good kid and knew, without being told, what a reasonable hour was.

When he came home, we talked about college and how he needed to apply because the deadlines were coming. I wanted Mikey to have the opportunity to go to college, so I asked him to apply to four different schools. Mikey knew that he did not have to go away to college if he chose not to. He knew that I just wanted him to apply so the doors would be open for him. He knew that if he was accepted, the choice was his. He surprised me by saying that a teacher, I can almost guess who, had already helped him with his applications. All he had to do was download the applications on the computer and fill them out. He decided to do it that night. I am sure his decision to get it out of the way was to make me happy so I would stop ragging him. When he finished his first application, he hollered for the credit card so he could pay the fees. It was late, and I could tell my little man was tired. I suggested he save the file and pay in the morning. He smiled a "thank God" smile, and a few moments later, he headed for his room. I can still hear his sweet voice as he said, "Good night, Mom, I love you."

Tuesday morning, November 20, I woke up to the same five-thirty alarm screaming at me, but I hopped out of bed with a little more zest. I was eager to get to work, do the eight hours, and start my minivacation. At six forty-five in the morning, I passed by Mikey's bedroom door. I was going to knock and wake him up a little early but changed my mind. He was up late the night before and needed the extra fifteen minutes of rest. As I was leaving for work, I reminded my husband to wake Mikey up at seven o'clock and, if he had time, give him the credit card so he could pay the application fees.

Mikey, very much like his mom, was rushing around and did not have time to finish the applications. He told his dad he'd finish over Thanksgiving break. As he left for school, Dad warned him to be careful on "that" road. Mikey knew he was talking about Neroly Road. It was a narrow country road with a sharp curve and an uneven shoulder that was always full of potholes and loose gravel. I say "was" because the road no longer exists. It has been realigned due to a new housing development that is being built. Every morning, his dad would tell him the same thing as Mikey walked out the door. "Mikey, if you go off 'that' road, don't try to get back on. With all those potholes, you might overcorrect and be thrown into the next lane. It's best to keep going into the apple orchard and come to a stop." Mikey would reply, "I know, Dad!"

On the way to work, I thought about the funeral that was to take place at our church. I made a mental note of the time (1:00 p.m.) and wrestled with the idea of leaving work early so that I could attend. I had missed so much work the year before. Twice I travel to Maryland from California. My mom died suddenly in August 2000 and, six weeks later, my sister died of multiple myeloma. I was taking a vacation day the next day, which would leave me with little vacation time left on the books. My husband was not well, and I knew I needed to save time in the event of an emergency. I still toyed with the idea of leaving early. I only needed to take four hours off. Surely, I could spare the time.

At work, we were served a catered breakfast to celebrate Thanksgiving. I did not enjoy the food and felt ungrateful. I was restless and had a hard time concentrating. I kept watching the clock. Time was passing, and I was still undecided about leaving work. At 10:15 a.m., my friend, Melchia, and I took our usual walk during morning break. I thought a brisk walk would help calm me down. Later that morning, I saw a helicopter but was not sure of the time. I remember when I looked up, I saw a big cross on the belly. It looked like it was heading in the direction of John Muir Hospital. I silently prayed.

Meanwhile, at Freedom High School, Mikey and his best friend, Joel, were in the process of planning an activity for the Christmas fundraiser. The boys ran into Mr. Amaro's classroom, announcing that they needed to make a great big, gigantic tennis ball. When Mr. Amaro, their tennis coach, questioned why, they explained that they were going to cut out targets so the kids could throw bean bags through them. The boys were bubbling over with excitement because they just knew, without a doubt, that their activity was going to bring in "thousands" of dollars for the needy families.

Mr. Amaro looked at his watch, noticed that it was 9:42 a.m., and told the boys he had an English class to teach in a few minutes. He asked them to come back later so they could talk about it further. "Later" was never to come. Meeting up with Brandon, another close friend, the three seniors decided to leave the school grounds to grab hamburgers for lunch.

A mom driving an older large-sized van was taking her daughter to school. She was going the speed limit of forty-five miles per hour. Taking the curve at twenty-eight to thirty miles per hour, Joel saw the van and swerved to the right. His right tire went off the road onto the shoulder. He overcorrected and was thrown into the other lane. Trying to avoid an accident, he overcorrected again, and his car slid sideways into the oncoming van. At approximately ten twenty-five in the morning, it was dispatched over the radio that there was a horrific accident on Neroly Road, just a half mile from Freedom High School.

A local pastor heard not one or two, but three sirens go off, and he began to pray.

Marc, our neighbor, is a paramedic/firefighter and was on another call when he heard the Oakley accident being dispatched over the ambulance radio. He instantly thought of Mikey and got an uneasy feeling. He said he got a sick feeling deep in the pit of his stomach, and his world seemed to slow down. He called his supervisor and asked, "Please tell me that there was not a maroon truck involved." His supervisor told him no. He said it was a van and a white Honda CRX. It appeared to be a head-on collision. One fatality, one taken to Sutter Delta Hospital, and the third boy was critical and being transported by Reach Air Ambulance to John Muir Trauma Center. Marc was relieved to hear that Mikey's truck was not involved and did not give the white Honda a second thought, but he still had an uneasy feeling that he could not shake.

On his way back to the station, he decided to pull over and call our house. Buddy, my oldest son, answered the phone, and he was obviously shaken up. Marc cautiously asked, "Hey, bro, Mikey didn't happen to come home for lunch, did he?" Buddy told him what his gut instinct already knew, and Marc said that was when his world came to a stop. He called his wife, Tanya, and raced to the hospital, attempting to get there before me. At one point, he clocked himself going over one hundred miles per hour. He knew Mikey's condition and was desperate to get to the hospital. He did not want me to be alone.

When Marc told Tanya the news, she said her blood ran cold. She was in no condition to drive, so a coworker drove her home. Once she pulled herself together, she went to our house to be with my husband and drive him to the hospital. The two of them share a special bond like that of a father and daughter. Her presence gave him great comfort.

Freedom High School was in turmoil. The news of the accident traveled fast, and even before it was announced, the kids already knew that Joel had died and Mikey was critical. Kids came together, crying and hugging one another as they gathered in private little huddles. They joined together in hallways, classrooms, and in the quad to comfort one another. Students were on cell phones calling their moms, and many mothers came to the school to await the news with their children. Rosy and Stephanie, two special girls in Mikey's life, were in separate rooms as they waited for their moms. Both girls were hysterical. The students were told not to leave school grounds, but several of the boys left anyways and came to our house to get Buddy. An officer escorted them through town so they could get to the freeway safely as they rushed to the hospital.

At noon, having finally decided not to attend the funeral, I went to the kitchen to eat lunch with my coworkers. That was unusual for me because I usually left the office to sit in the courtyard during lunch. At 12:20 p.m., I returned to my desk for a brief moment. My phone was ringing. I poked my head around the corner and reminded the receptionist that I was still at lunch. She said it was my husband. Silent alarms went off. My husband never calls me at work. When I answered the phone and heard his voice, I knew that something terrible had happened. With a gentle, quivering voice, he told me that I needed to go to John Muir Hospital. I asked what was wrong, and he started to cry. In a broken voice, barely above a whisper, he managed to tell me that Mikey had been in an accident. My heart sank, and that was all I heard. That was all I had time to hear. My precious Mikey was hurt, and I needed to get to him. I hung up the phone and ran across the office to tell my manager that I was leaving. Screaming out that my Mikey was in an accident, she could see that I was in no condition to drive and wanted to take me to the hospital, but I declined her offer. I had no time to waste. I had to get to the hospital to be with my Mikey. I didn't want to spare the seconds it would take for her to gather her purse. In fear and desperation, I ran. I ran out of the office and down the stairwell. I ran across the courtyard into the parking garage. I jumped into my truck, and I think I began driving before I even shut the door.

The hospital is about fifteen miles from my office, but the drive seemed to take forever. All the way there I prayed. I had no idea what condition Mikey was in, but I sensed it was not good because he was taken to the trauma center. What I did not know, at the time, was that he was flown by helicopter. His condition was critical, and he was dying. As I was rushing to be by my precious son's side, he was dying. I prayed,

I prayed hard. Over and over again, I asked God to be with my baby. I remember looking at the clock. The hour was 12:52 p.m., and I was just minutes from the hospital. I remember calling out to Mikey, "I'm coming, Mikey. Mommy's almost there, baby!" I reached the hospital and pulled into the first parking spot that came into view and ran.

Entering the ER registration area, I frantically announced who I was. The young lady said she would go tell the doctor that I had arrived, and she rushed into the emergency room. Her expression and fast pace alarmed me, and I began to panic. I wanted to run into the emergency room with her, but I just stood there. I was paralyzed with fear. I could feel my heart pounding, and my throat felt like it was closed shut. I had a hard time breathing. I tried to pray, but the only audible words that would come out were, "Oh my God, oh my God, oh sweet Jesus!" A few moments later, the same lady came back and asked me to follow her to the family room. She unlocked the door and told me that the supervising nurse would be with me soon. Then she left. She left me in the dreaded family room, and I was all alone. I knew the news was going to be bad, so very bad. I fell to my knees and cried out to God. A thick layer of fog seemed to wrap around me, and I felt the presence of God. His Holy Spirit filled that room and renewed me with a strength that only He could provide. Although the fear remained, I was able to take control of my emotions, so by the time the supervising nurse arrived, I had managed to compose myself and was standing once again. She was a kind woman and spoke to me in a soft, loving tone. I don't remember her exact words. I heard "critical condition," "doctor will be in soon," getting my son ready for ICU. I remember feeling relief that he was still alive. I asked to use the phone. I needed to call my church. Mikey needed prayer. He needed it fast! As I dialed the number, I was concerned that no one would answer the phone because of the funeral. Someone, I don't remember who, answered the phone. I remember talking to Pastor Marc, our youth pastor. He said he was leaving immediately and would be there as soon as possible.

Only minutes had passed from the time I reached the hospital to the time I spoke to Pastor Marc. It seemed like hours. The doctor came to talk with me. By now, I was in a state of shock, and the doctor's voice seemed to be coming from a distance. It sounded like he was talking to me from the other end of a tunnel. As he spoke, I was only able to grasp partial sentences. Once again, I do not remember the exact words. I heard auto accident, half mile from the school, thirty miles an hour, severe head trauma. I do remember him telling me that they had done a CAT scan. He had a massive head injury and had not moved the entire time he had been in the hospital. He told me that Mikey's pupils were 100 percent dilated. I knew that was bad. I knew it meant brain dead, but I searched the doctor's face for hope and said, "That's good, right?" He told me no and talked some more. I don't remember what he said. I asked if Mikey was going to be okay. I could see the pain in his eyes, and I knew his answer. He gently told me that my son died at one o'clock. Suddenly, I felt sick. I told the nurse, and she gave me a trash can. Waves of nausea swept through my stomach. I wanted to throw up, but I couldn't. I could not believe what I have heard. My beautiful baby was gone. There was that 1:00 p.m. again. Ironic how that time had been the focus of my whole morning.

The doctor stayed a while and just sat quietly. Then he left, and I was alone with the nurse. I remember thinking, "What now? Dear God, what now? Does my husband know Mikey died? Where is Buddy?" I picked up the phone and called my church. I needed prayer! By now, I was sure that the service had started. Surely no one was going to answer the phone now. Through the grace of God, the church secretary, my close friend Carolyn Trapanese, answered the phone. Her sweet voice was music to my ears and gave me more comfort than she will ever be able to comprehend. Months later, Carolyn shared that when she answered the phone, all I said was, "My baby's gone. Carolyn, my baby's gone!" She rushed to the hospital and arrived shortly after Pastor Marc's arrival.

From that point on, everything became fuzzy, and time had no beginning or ending. The nausea was still present. I wanted to scream with hysteria, but all that would come were rivers of silent tears. There was a buzzing sound in my ears, and a tingling sensation rushed through my body. I became numb. I could not believe that Mikey had died. How could this be happening to my family?

Someone asked what my religion was. I remember saying I was Pentecostal. I was told that there was not a pastor in the hospital, but a priest was there. At that moment, I did not care if a rabbi came to pray with me. I just wanted a man of God, and I wanted him right then. When the priest entered the family room, I remember feeling a sense of relief; but at the same time, I was taken aback by his tall stature and brilliant blue eyes. As long as I live, I will always remember those blue eyes. I saw kindness, and I saw pain. I saw Jesus. Maybe what I was seeing was my own pain reflecting from his eyes like a mirror. I come from a loving church where hugs come naturally. The priest seemed reserved, and although I was grateful that he was there, I wanted my Pastor Reynolds. I needed a hug. The priest asked if I wanted to see Mikey. Yes, I wanted to see my baby. Someone warned me that he was going to look different. They told me the tubes have been disconnected, but he still had part of the respirator in his mouth.

As I entered the room, I was taken by surprise at how big he looked lying there. I was shocked and sobbed, "He looks like a man." I have no idea where that comment came from. Maybe I meant to say, "When did my little boy grow up?" I approached my son slowly. His head was fully bandaged, and his beautiful face was already bruised on the right side. Although his body was traumatized, he looked like he was sleeping. I looked over at the priest and saw his blue eyes filled with sorrow. He stayed with me for a while then recommended that I spend time alone with my son, and he quietly left the room.

I stood beside Mikey and just stared. I felt as though Mikey knew it was okay for him to "let go" once I arrived at the hospital. I was sure he waited for me. I looked up at the ceiling as though his spirit were lingering above. I did not feel his presence and knew that my son was absent from his body. Although I knew that he was present with the Lord, I wanted to climb into the hospital bed and cuddle him, but I was afraid of what the hospital staff would think if they saw me. I wanted to gently touch his precious cheek, but I was afraid I'd hurt him. Silly, he was dead. How could I hurt him? I lifted the sheet and saw a small superficial wound on his leg. I wanted to scream that he needed a bandage. I wanted to pick him up and take him home, home to my house, not God's house. Guilt began to torment me. It should have been me lying there, not my son. His life was just beginning. Mine was half over. I felt as though I had betrayed my son. I was always harder on him than my older son. My expectations were always higher. I used to promise him that someday he would look at a little old lady, his momma, and he would thank me. Instead, I was looking at a young man that did not have the chance to experience the fullness of manhood. Before I left the room, it was me who thanked him. I thanked him for being my son and for all the joy he had given me. I did not say good-bye. In our house, there are no good-byes. Regardless of the situation, we know we will see one another again, if not here on earth, then in heaven with our Heavenly Father.

In elementary school, Mikey's best friend was Joey. His mother, Cheryl, has worked at John Muir in the ER room for years. Someone asked if I wanted her to come be with me. I assumed she was there in the hospital, so I said yes. I waited for her. I could not understand what was taking her so long. Minutes seemed like hours, and as strange as it may sound, hours seemed like minutes. I had no sense of time. She finally came to sit with me in the family room. I don't know if we talked. I don't even know if we hugged. So many moments are a blur. I do know that having Cheryl present gave me comfort. She was a familiar face in a sad place. She was a connection to memories gone by. In just seconds, she was an acquaintance that I suddenly took possession of and claimed as my best friend. I fed off her strength. I was to later learn that Cheryl was not working that tragic day. She was at home when she heard about the accident.

My son, Buddy, arrived safely with several friends. He came to me and held me tight. I could feel him trembling, and I knew that he too was in shock. I'm not sure, but I think it was Buddy who told me that Joel died instantly in the accident. I was to learn that Brandon survived and was at a different hospital, being treated for his injuries. My husband arrived with Tanya. I wanted to reach out to him. I wanted to wrap my arms around him and hold him tight, but I couldn't. I knew that if I did, we both would fall apart, so I kept my distance.

News of the accident traveled fast, and soon there were numerous young adults outside the hospital doors, all of them coming together to support one another. Many were taking off from work to be there for Buddy. One of Buddy's lifelong friends came into the family room and totally fell apart. My own pain was put aside as I reached out to hold him. It broke my heart to see him so devastated. All I could do was hold him and tell him that Mikey was okay now. He was with Jesus where there is no suffering. The coroner wanted to take Mikey's body, but I asked to let those that came be able to spend a few minutes alone with Mikey. I felt it was good for closure, and many of Mikey's friends did spend time alone with him. I do not know if Buddy did. I never asked.

Brenda, Joel's mom, was working when a cell phone started ringing. A lady who was working in the flower department realized it was hers and answered it. It was her daughter. When the lady finished talking to her daughter, she looked at Brenda and said, "Oh my God, have you heard about the accident?"

"No, what accident?" Brenda asked.

"The one on Neroly Road. Couple of kids from Freedom. My daughter just told me that one died and the other was critical."

Although it didn't even cross Brenda's mind that one of the kids could be Joel, she was concerned and asked who the kids were. The lady didn't know so she called her daughter back and asked the names. Unaware of Brenda's last name, she told Brenda that it was Mike Kelly and Joel Richards. Shocked at what she had just heard, Brenda raced out of the store and desperately called her husband who was already on his way to her.

Brandon's mom, Linda, is a school teacher at one of the local elementary schools. She was in her classroom when the office manager came to tell her she needed to go to the office. There was a phone call waiting for her. It was the hospital. She was told her son was there in the ER. He had been in an accident and brought in on a backboard. Linda was informed that Brandon was a passenger, the driver was deceased, and another boy airlifted.

They would not release any names. Realizing how bad the accident was, Linda asked if Brandon was conscious and was told yes. She was told that the doctor was still with him and that he was upset—she needed to come right away!

When she stood up, she felt her legs buckle. The school secretary grabbed her and had her sit back down then went to get Linda's purse and keys.

She remembers, when she arrived at the hospital, there was a priest there. She overheard a staff employee tell the priest, "He's not here, he was taken to John Muir." Becoming more anxious, she was grateful when a nurse finally took her to Brandon and saw him sitting up in the hospital bed. He took one look at his mom and said, "Mom, Joel is dead!" He told her that Mikey was the other person in the car and insisted that he needed to leave. He wanted to be with him.

When Brandon was discharged, Linda had to take him home to get him a shirt because his was cut off in ER. As Brandon went to get his shirt, Linda called John Muir and was told that Mikey had passed away. Brandon was devastated. He just lost two of his closest friends.

Freedom High School announced around two forty-five in the afternoon that Mike Kelly and Joel Richards had died. The teachers and staff cried with the students, all grieving the loss of two young lives.

At three o'clock, when we left the hospital, I thought about my coworker and closest friend, Melchia, and I called my manager, Marilyn Haynes. I wanted her to tell Melchia about Mikey before she heard the news from someone else. I did not have the strength to tell her myself. Melchia was at my door within hours and was to be there for me in the weeks to come. Every day after work, she came to comfort me. Sometimes we talked and other times she just sat beside me. No words needed to be spoken. The comfort was there. That was all I needed.

Tanya drove my husband and me home, and once again my heart was shattered when she cried out loud that she did not know what she was going to tell her babies. Jacob and Kamryn were so young. How was she going to explain to them that their Mikey was no longer going to be around to play with them or tell them scary stories? He was no longer going to do the "goodnight dance" when it was time for them to go to bed. They loved him so. He was like a big brother to them. I prayed to God and asked Him to anoint Marc and Tanya with wisdom so that they would have the right collection of words to explain why their Mikey went to live with Jesus.

When we arrived home and walked into the house, the first thing I saw was Mikey's surfboard propped up against the wall. My first thought was, "I'll give it to Joel." Then I remembered that Joel had died too. It saddened me that Joel had died, but I felt comfort knowing that the boys were together.

My next thought was that people would be coming. Lots of people! I looked at Tanya and asked if she would help me clean my house. I had just cleaned it Saturday, so I knew it would not take long. As we moved clutter from one spot to another, we sobbed. By 6:00 p.m., my house was overflowing with people of all ages who had not come to judge the cleanliness of our home. They came to share our grief and to give love. It appeared that the whole town of Oakley came to mourn the loss of Mikey and Joel, and in the midst of it all was my comforter, Jesus Christ.

On a cold day in January 1984, I walked into the hospital and gave birth to a beautiful baby boy. My whole life changed the day he was born. Seventeen years later, on a brisk day in November 2001, I walked out of the hospital with empty arms, and my whole life was to change again. Every fiber of my being was traumatized and broken. I had a hole in my heart the size of the Grand Canyon, if not bigger, and I thought that I too would die from the horrific pain. I had no idea how I was going to get through Mikey's death in the days to come, but I knew that the only way I would survive was to trust in God. Because of His promise of eternal life, I was able to embrace hope, and with His mercy I continued to breathe through my darkest hour.

*May the God of hope fill you
With all joy and peace as you trust
in Him, so that you may overflow
with hope by the power of the
Holy Spirit.*

––Romans 15:13

Mavericks

A few months after Mikey died, I had a dream that a young man and I were running along the beach. I was wearing my gray sweats, and we were laughing and laughing. There was no pain. I was free of grief and sorrow. There were no tears, just this incredible feeling of peace and an abundance of joy. How I have missed that sweet, sweet laughter.

Suddenly, the clouds turned dark, and a storm fell upon us. The laughter was ripped away and replaced by indescribable fear. I saw a man standing in water up to his thighs. This faceless man was holding out his hand and calling out to me. He was telling me to come and follow him into the water. I did not know who he was.

I don't remember the sound of his voice, and I never saw his face. I was consumed with fear, but I went to join him. As I drew closer to him, my fear began to recede. It was replaced with trust. The storm grew fierce, and a huge tidal wave was approaching. The man said that when the tidal wave came, I needed to dive into the swell of the wave and not let it crash upon me. I did as instructed and dove into the swell as it reached the peak of the breaking point.

I was deep in the water when I heard his voice. He told me to swim upward so that I would not drown. I trusted him and swam upward. I can still feel the tug of the current, pulling me as I struggled to reach the surface. I still feel the cool sensation of the water against my flesh. I can still feel how safe I felt and the tremendous peace along with a blanket of comfort that surrounded me. When I reached the surface, the storm had passed, and the sky was blue again. I could no longer see the man, but I could feel his presence.

I woke up, and the details of the dream were so vivid that it felt as though it really happened. I did not need to analyze the dream. I knew the message that God conveyed to me. As God held out his loving hand, He was asking me to trust in Him and to follow Him. He was letting me know that He was with me and that although I was in the midst of a storm, He would guide me through it and I would not drown. The dream renewed my hope and has become a source of strength for me.

I find it interesting that my hope was restored through such a dream. The ocean has always been a place of comfort to my family and me.

When our sons were quite young, my husband and I would take them to the pumpkin patches in Half Moon Bay every year. We would visit every pumpkin patch until the boys found the pumpkin they wanted. Mikey's pumpkin had to be perfectly round, and there could be no defects. Buddy always selected an oblong specimen and a few dings here, and there was no big deal to him. Before leaving, we would stop at a beach in El Granada and let the boys play in the sand. My husband, Bud, grew up on the Gulf Coast of Galveston, Texas. I grew up on the Atlantic Coast in Maryland. We both love the ocean, so it was a delight to introduce our sons to California's Pacific Ocean.

We began to make trips to Half Moon Bay as often as time would allow. On sunny days, we would pack up the fishing gear and all the "beach stuff," such as sand bucket, towels, sunscreen, and lots of goodies to eat. If it was a windy day, we would take kites. Sometimes our friend would lend us his little camper and we would camp out. What a sight that must have been. At the campsite in El Granada, there were always expensive-looking RVs and fancy tents, all neatly lined up side by side. Then in the Kellys would come, towing an early 1950s model camper.

The camper had grass and weeds growing on the outside because it had been parked in a field for many years. The inside was worn but clean, so we didn't care. It served our purpose: just the four of us out on a family outing having a good time. We would fish, eat, build sand castles, eat, take walks, eat, search for seashells, and yes, you guessed it, eat some more. I can still hear my sons giggle as their tiny feet chased the waves. Life was simple then. We were blessed.

Eventually, we graduated to a twenty-eight-foot houseboat and would spend most weekends cruising the delta near Antioch. We would anchor the boat and barbecue with friends. Both boys loved the water. Buddy was obedient and adhered to the rules. Mikey was a holy terror. So long as he could be in the water he was fine. He could not get enough of the wet stuff. With life vest securely strapped on, he was constantly trying to jump overboard. He had no fear. Bud did everything he could to keep him safe. He attached netting around the guardrails that surrounded the boat, and when that didn't work, he replaced the netting with canvas. When Buddy was five and Mikey two, Bud decided to sell the boat, buy a house, and settle down. Bud often teased that when all you hear is the bullfrogs and your wife fussing at the kids, it was time to sell.

At the time, Bud was putting in many hours working at the naval weapons station as a civilian. While he worked, I would pack up the boys and all the "beach stuff" and head for the ocean. Soon, the sand buckets were replaced with boogie boards, and McDonald's happy meals were introduced. Buddy enjoyed the ocean, but Mikey developed a passion for it. He never seemed to get enough. He lived and breathed for the moments that he could be there.

When Bud's work slowed down, he would join us on occasional trips to Half Moon Bay. Sometimes the boys would fish with their dad, but most of the time we would end up on the beach watching Mikey as he played in the freezing water. He never complained of being cold, pretended that he wasn't tired, and he fussed when it was time to leave.

I don't know why or when, but the time came when it was only Mikey and me who would take trips to the ocean. Buddy would join us if we were going only for a few hours, but that seldom was the case. A few hours on the beach just wasn't enough time for the two of us. With a boogie board in tow and a few bucks in our pockets, we would take off after telling Dad that we'd be home early. He would just nod his head, knowing full well that he wouldn't see us again until six or seven that night. All the way to Half Moon Bay we'd grin from ear to ear. Sometimes Mikey would talk nonstop about stuff, and other times we'd sing some of the old songs that I remembered from my younger years. I can still hear Mikey's laugh as I sang "Jeremiah Was a Bullfrog" and "The Monster Mash."

Sometimes an old song would come over the radio, and he would turn up the volume really loud and just smile. At times like that, we didn't need to speak. I would return Mikey's smile, and my heart would be full of joy. I knew it was his way of saying, "I remember, Mom. This is for you!"

As the years passed, Mikey's passion for the ocean grew even stronger. He read everything he could get his hands on that pertained to the ocean or surfing. He studied all the safety aspects and knew what to do in the event that he got caught up in a riptide. He quizzed me often, and I always flunked. Mikey would puff up like a rooster, and his eyes would twinkle. He loved the fact that he was teaching me.

When Mikey started high school, a special young girl named Rosa "Rosy" Stevens entered his life. The two of them became close, and as they grew, so did their love for one another. The first time Mikey asked if Rosy could go to the ocean with us, he was softspoken and gentle. He knew that these trips were our special time together, and he was not sure how I would respond. Mikey was sensitive about my feelings, and I was sensitive about his needs. I had no problem with the two of us becoming a threesome. We continued to have fun at the beach.

The two of them would wander off to spend time alone, but they would return after a short while. I loved watching them chase one another along the beach. I loved hearing them laugh and seeing them talking quietly as they shared their feelings. Their love for one another was sweet and innocent and so genuine. After a day on the beach, we would stop at McDonald's for a quick meal, which had now become a tradition.

Mikey chose not to go surfing when Rosy came along on the trips. He couldn't bear to be separated from her, so when he wanted to go in the water, he didn't invite her. He knew that once he started surfing, he would continue until it was time to return home. Mikey purchased his first surfboard at a little shop in Half Moon Bay. He had saved for his board and was very proud of his purchase. He expressed who he was by the stickers he placed on his board. I do believe that out of all the material things that Mikey owned, he treasured his board the most. He took good care of it, always making sure to rinse off the saltwater when he got home, no matter how tired he was.

Surfing became more than a sport to Mikey. It became a challenge, and his dream was to master it someday. Mikey discovered a place in Half Moon Bay called "Mavericks," and every time we went to the ocean, we had to stop there. Mavericks is a beautiful place. Sometimes the tide was so low that we could climb around the rocks and up the cliff to get to the other side. The view was breathtaking.

World-champion surfers surf at Mavericks. Often, I would get home from work, and Mikey would be raring to go. His dad told him that he had heard on the news that the surf was high, and the champions were there. Five thirty in the afternoon, in the midst of rush hour, we'd take off hoping to arrive in time to get a glimpse of them. We never did make it in time. They would always be gone, not even a trace that they had been there. But the waves would still be big, and Mikey would say, "May as well hang out for a while since we came all this way." He was so good-natured and easygoing, making the best of every situation. Mavericks became Mikey's mountain, and he dreamed of the day that he would be able to surf there.

Sometimes we would make our trip just to be by the ocean. We would drive along the coast and explore various beaches, but we always returned to the place that stole Mikey's heart, Mavericks. There were moments when we would walk along the shoreline in silence, each in our own little world, thinking our private thoughts. Just being at the ocean was words enough for us.

Then there were moments when we would pour our hearts out to one another. We talked about school, work, family, friends, and life in general. We shared our feelings. We shared our joys and our disappointments. We were honest with one another, even if we knew there were things that the other really didn't want to hear.

Mikey and I did a lot of dreaming there. Long-term goals were made. Our futures were being planned. Toward the end of Mikey's life, we talked about God and what he was doing in my life. Our conversations were deep and heartwarming, honest and sweet. There was joy within our hearts, and peace was ever present. I will forever cherish those moments.

Our final trip to the ocean together was three weeks before the accident. Mikey seemed desperate to get there, and he kept watching the clock along the way. The traffic was heavy, and it took over two hours to get there. Mikey was restless and anxious. When we reached Half Moon Bay, we discovered what created the traffic problems: the annual pumpkin festival. Amazing how fate works in our lives. Mikey's first and final visit to the ocean, with me, was during the pumpkin festival. We had gone full circle. God allowed this completeness to take place.

When we got to El Granada, Mikey grabbed his board and went straight into the water. Usually, I couldn't get him to come out of the water when it would be time to leave. I would go stand by the shoreline and wave until I got his attention, and he would hold up his index finger. I thought that meant "one minute." His minute would be a really long minute, and I would find myself becoming irritated with him. One day, I finally spoke to him about "his minute," and he looked at me in disbelief. He could not believe that after all this time, I didn't know what his sign meant. He thought I knew that it meant one more wave. He apologized, and I learned to flag him down thirty minutes before it was time to go. It wasn't long before he caught on and started holding up two fingers.

Our last trip together was different from all the others. I didn't have to flag him down. He was only in the water for a short while when he came out and announced that he was ready to leave. I was surprised and asked what was up. He said the surf sucked and he wasn't having any fun. Waves looked fine to me, but what do I know? I asked if he wanted to stop and grab a burrito, and again I was surprised that he said no. Mikey was restless. I knew something was wrong, and it was driving me nuts. This was not the Mikey I knew. The Mikey I knew loved catching a good wave, but had no problem just floating around on his board. The Mikey I knew loved burritos and would not turn one down.

When he asked if I thought we'd be home by four thirty and I said "no way," I heard a little drawn-out "ooooooh." That is when he told me about his date. He and Rosy had broken up over the summer, and in the fall, he had met a girl named Stephanie Grelli. He made a date with her on the same day he had plans with me. I teased him and said that he should never make two dates on the same day. He said he thought we would be home in time. So that was the reason for his restlessness and the pitiful waves. When I mentioned that we could have gone another time, he made the comment that he didn't want to break our plans. He wanted to go with me. Needless to say, Mikey was two hours late for his date, and Steph was not a happy camper because she thought he had stood her up.

When Steph was to learn that Mikey went to the ocean with his mom, she thought that was so sweet and she couldn't remain upset. More dates with Steph were to come, and he soon shared Mavericks with her. Their time together was short, but the quality time was good. Mikey's heart was broken when he and Rosy broke up. Steph brought joy back into his life.

Through his relationship with Steph, an old friendship was rekindled. Mikey and Joey were best friends all through elementary school. Shortly after Mikey died, Joey came to our home and sat in Mikey's room with me. He looked all around and pointed out exactly where Mikey's things used to be, and he shared his memories of Mikey with me. Although my wound was still raw, Joey helped to soothe the pain. Today, Joey is able to reflect on their good times, which is a blessing.

Mavericks holds a special place in my heart. It's where I go to find my peace, but the ride home is always difficult. No matter who I am with, I feel the void. I always yearn for my Mikey on the way home. This is when I miss him the most.

The ride home, with Mikey, served up my sweetest memories. I would be cold, and Mikey would be hot. He was my little polar bear. I'd turn on the heat and point the vents toward me, and he'd roll down his window. We always stopped at McDonald's, but it had become the place for restroom use only. The summer before Mikey died, he had found a little Mexican hole-in-the-wall that served a mean burrito. Mikey would be starving, thirsty, and relaxed to the point where he was sleepy. We would stop for a burrito, and he would gobble it down, enjoying every bite. On the drive home we would talk, but just for a little while. I would be talking, and when he didn't answer, I'd look over and my son, now all grown up, would be asleep. I would reach over and gently stroke his sweet face; he would open his eyes and give me a big smile. I always told him that he brought joy to my heart, and that tired little smile would grow even more beautiful.

I marveled at the beauty of Mikey and treasured him. I knew how deeply I loved him. I did not think it possible to love him more. Not only did I love him, but I truly liked him. Mikey was a blessing in my life.

I miss my walks with Mikey at the ocean. I miss our mutual moments of silence. I miss the laughter we shared and the dreams we dreamed. I miss climbing the rocks at Mavericks and hearing him say, "Come on, ole woman, you can do it!" while holding his hand out to me so I wouldn't fall. I miss the commitments that rain or shine, we were going. I miss leaving home with my son, and it would be raining so hard my husband was sure we were both nuts for going to the ocean. I miss arriving there, and the sky would be blue and the sun would be shining. I miss hearing Mikey's statements that he knew it, he just knew that it would be sunny when we arrived at the shore. I miss the times Mikey and I would look at each other and say, "I need to go clean the cobwebs out of my head, how about you?" I miss the two of us trying to dig up enough gas money when we were broke but so desperate to get there. I miss our ride home and that look of peace and contentment on his face. I miss the "sorry we're late" when we got home and my husband's response that he knew we would be. I miss my son!

Returning to the place Mikey loved was a journey that my son, Buddy, and I believed we needed to take. We knew it was going to be painful, but I don't think either of us realized how excruciating the pain would be. How could we have known? We had just buried the heartbeat of our family. Surely there would be no greater pain.

Our first trip to Mavericks was about a month after Mikey's accident. We were still in a state of shock. The unimaginable has happened to our family. Mikey's death had left us feeling empty. There was an incredible void, and our souls felt little joy. We were zombies going through the rituals of everyday life, existing but not living. We drove to the ocean in silence. My mind kept wandering, and I was unable to focus on anything. When I look back, I am amazed that we arrived safely at our seaside destination.

As we drew closer to the coast, heaviness weighed upon me. My eyes started to tear up, and everything became blurry. I fought hard to keep from crying out. I kept swallowing a lot and clearing my throat. I prayed to God for strength. I wanted to be strong for Buddy, my oldest and only surviving son. I needed to control my emotions so that I could be there for him. I looked over at him, and I saw such sadness. I wanted to mend his broken heart and take away his pain. I wanted to turn back the clock and give him back his brother. I hated death and what it represented. I wanted our Mikey back.

The impact of Mikey's death reached the depth of my soul at the first glimpse of the ocean. Waves of turmoil swept through my body, and the horror of his death overcame me. Denial became reality, and I lost control of all the emotions that I had worked so hard to control since his death. The tears poured down my cheeks in streams. I kept trying to wipe them away, but they just kept flowing. I could hear Buddy sobbing, and when I glanced at him, he was leaning against the door looking out at the ocean. Rivers of tears were pouring down his face. I could feel his pain. I wanted to give him words of comfort, but I could find no words, so I said nothing. Truth is, there were no words that could have comforted him. Just being in the presence of one another and going through this journey together was enough. It was then that I realized that it was okay for him to see me cry. My tears gave him permission to cry too.

By the time we reached Half Moon Bay, we had managed to compose our emotions and put on another new mask in order to disguise our feelings. As we walked along the familiar path that led to Mavericks, there was none of the conversation that usually took place. The laughter was absent as well as the joyful bounce in our steps. Everything looked gray, and the fog seemed to wrap itself around us. It must have been cold, but we were too numb to feel the coldness. I don't remember feeling the wind that frequently visits Mavericks during the winter months.

When we rounded the final curve in the path and the full view of Mavericks came into sight, the wind was knocked out of me. I had to gasp for breath. That heavy feeling snuck its way back inside me and surrounded my heart.

There was tightness in my chest. A lump was in my throat, and the more I tried to swallow, the bigger it got, making it more difficult for me to breathe. I silently cried out to God and prayed for help. He slowly washed away my anxiety and renewed my strength.

I began to smell the fragrance of the ocean and hear the sounds of the crashing waves. The pungent smell of the sea kelp that used to offend me became inviting. The foghorn in the distance was music to my ears. Mikey's presence was powerful. The essence of his being was profound. Visions of him were everywhere. I could see him in his board shorts, running around chasing us with sea kelp. I could see his sweet smile and hear his laughter. I could see him standing tall with his hands in his pockets gazing out into the ocean dreaming his dreams. I longed for Mikey. I realized that he would never walk along the beach with me again, but I knew his spirit would always be with me.

Buddy and I walked slowly along the beach, stopping every so often to pick up a shell. We headed for the rocks that we could climb. The tide was high, so we could not climb far. Buddy brought Mikey's favorite roses (fire and ice), and in his honor, he gently tossed them into the ocean, one by one. It was a beautiful moment, and we watched as the ocean carried them out to sea. As we were leaving, we noticed that two of the roses had drifted back toward us and had connected, one crossing the other. It was symbolic, and in the midst of all that sadness, we were able to smile. One rose represented Mikey, and the other represented his best friend Joel, who also died in the accident. I believe that God was sending us a little message letting us know that the boys were okay. They were together, with Him, for eternity.

When I left Mavericks, my heart was still heavy, but I carried with me the comfort of knowing that I had overcome any fears I had about returning. I did not want to close the door to a place that Mikey loved so much. I wanted to continue to walk along the beach and pick up shells again, even the broken ones that Mikey thought were just as lovely. I did not want to stay away and not experience the peace that we shared there. I did not want to forget the sounds of the crashing waves and the cries of the seagulls. I wanted to hear the foghorn in the distance again.

I did not want to forget Mikey's passion.

I have been back to the ocean many times since. It is where I go when I miss Mikey. It is where I go to say hello.

It is where I go to find my peace. Each time, God blesses me with a little message to let me know that he is with me. With each visit, I grow a little stronger. There is sorrow, but with sorrow there is joy. Sometimes there are tears, but beneath the tears there is a beautiful memory and a smile seems to follow.

Although I only see one set of footprints as I walk along the shoreline, I feel Mikey's presence through my memories. When evening falls, my footprints are washed away by the tide, but Mikey's footprints remain in my heart, never to be washed away. I do not grieve when I am at the ocean because there is no fear. There are only beautiful, sweet memories.

My prayer for you is that you too can go back to your special place that you shared with your loved one. I pray that you too will find the peace that I have found. The first time is so very painful, but know that God will be carrying you. Put your trust in Him. He will never abandon you. Our God is such a loving God. When you are weeping, He is weeping too.

You can receive your strength through Christ Jesus. You only need to open your heart, invite Him in, and allow Him to dwell within.

Seize The Moment

Written by Mikey Kelly -2001-

Surfing is a sport that I call mine. No one in my family goes into the water because it's about forty-five degrees. So I can get away from everyone for the entire day. To me, surfing is a form of art and self-expression.

First, you look at the person's board. What stickers are on it, or what pictures they have. On my surfboard, I have blue-and-purple flames. Then I put stickers from my favorite surf brand on it. Every day of my life, I express myself through surfing. Whether it's my clothing, what magazines I read, or even what I dream about at night, I am always involved in surfing.

One of the biggest dreams I have about the ocean is to become one with it. Not only to conquer it, but to make friends as well.

*Your word is a lamp to my feet
And a light to my path.*

—Psalm 119:105

Christmas

Mikey and Joel passed away two days before Thanksgiving and thirty-five days before Christmas. I wish I could share that I was able to give it all to God and continue on with an abundance of peace, but I can't. Truth be told, I was heartbroken and totally miserable. There was a real battle going on within my mind and soul. I wanted to die too! I wanted nothing to do with celebrating Thanksgiving. Two full Thanksgiving meals were given along with an abundance of food and desserts. My out-of-state family had to start freezing it all. I had no desire to eat or drink, and the more my family insisted I eat, the more nauseous I became. I tried though, I really did. I was grateful for family, and I was especially grateful that David, my husband's son, flew in from Arkansas. David brought comfort to Bud and Buddy, comfort I was unable to give. I was just too broken.

By the time Christmas arrived, I was a tiny bit better. At least I was functional enough to put on a mask long enough to run in stores, grab a few gifts, and run out as fast as I could. When I bumped into someone I knew, I smiled, said Merry Christmas and yes, I was okay. Okay? Okay? Really? I was far from okay, but it did seem to be the magic word to hush people up. The two reasons that kept me standing was my faith in God and determination to celebrate the birth of Christ for the love of my husband and son. I had to continue on for them because I wanted them to know that they were worthy and loved too. This was a great battle for me, as a Christian, to comprehend how I could have the joy of the Lord embedded within my soul but continue to feel so miserable and unhappy. I had a hard time separating the two. I was later to understand that joy and happiness were two separate emotions. It took me a while, but I managed to buy a small tree and drag it into the living room. That is as far as it got. I don't remember how many days it lay there before some of Buddy's friends noticed and came to decorate it for us. Although I was so unhappy, I felt great joy within, and I think I even attempted to make some hot chocolate. Without Jesus, I could not have felt that joy. He sent his army to help. What a wonderful blessing they were!

Christmas morning, I was so sad for Buddy. It just wasn't the same for him. I knew he felt the void with his little brother gone. They used to wake up superearly and sneak into the living room to raid their stockings. I do believe the stockings were their favorites.

On Christmas night, Kathy (Bud's daughter) and Vivian (Bud's granddaughter) flew in from Arkansas. They stayed until New Year's Eve, and this was a great time of healing for Bud. He adores his daughter. That is his baby girl!

The following Christmas wasn't much easier, but the good news is that we got through, and with each passing year we got stronger. I no longer had to put on a mask and fake happiness. I allowed myself to be exposed to as much Christmas as I could handle and stayed to myself when I have had enough. I gave myself permission to feel sad without bringing others down. I told myself that Mikey was worthy of every single tear!

Today, when you see a tear slipping down my check, think of it as a golden tear because it is not from sadness. One of God's gifts to me is being able to remember so many days gone by. Just when I think I have used up all my memories of Mikey and have no chance to make more, a memory would pop up. These memories are more precious than gold. Memories we did not plan to make. They were moments in life that just happened and years down the road became a memory. Memories that have turned sorrow into joy. Thank you, Jesus!

Train up a child in the way he should go; even when he is old he will not depart from it.

—Proverbs 22:6

Hamburgers, Tacos, Or Pizza

I woke up to the sprinkling of water and the muffled sound of someone crying. At first, the crying seemed to be coming from a distance, and then I realized that it was my husband, Bud. He was in the shower, and he was weeping. It broke my heart to hear him in so much distress. I wanted to go to him and give him comfort. Instead I rolled over, pulled the covers over my head, and pretended to be asleep. My husband needed his quiet time so that he could mourn. He too was suffering from a great loss. I had to respect his space so that he could work through his grief freely.

While lying in bed, I reflected on the relationship he had with Mikey. Like me, he expected a lot out of Mikey and set high standards for him to meet. Especially when it came to his education. He knew what his son was capable of and expected him to meet those capabilities. Like every other father and son, they had their share of battles, but I can honestly say there were very few. The greatest battle of all the issues he had were Mikey's little piles of clutter that seemed to take up residence throughout the house.

When it came to sports, he let the coaches do the coaching and never interfered. I don't ever remember him pushing Mikey to be bigger or better than the others. The important thing was for Mikey to do his best and have fun. He would always tell Mikey, "Just go out there and have a good time." He taught Mikey that it was all about attitude. Of course, he thought a little motivation was good for the spirit and would slip Mikey a few bucks for a job well done. It was one of those "shhhhh, Momma doesn't need to know about it" deals between father and son.

I'll always remember the day when I first found out about Bud's little motivations.

I got off work at the peak of rush hour and had to fight the gridlock of the commute traffic. I was my usual half-hour late and had to park what seemed to be a half mile away. As I walked toward the ballpark, I could hear the chanting of the crowd.

"Hey, batter, batter! Hey, batter, batter! Swing!"

Simultaneously, the crowd was hollering, "Come on, Mikey. You can do it, pal. Keep your eye on the ball!" When I heard the crowd screaming Mikey's name, I picked up my pace; and just as I reached the field, I heard the cracking sound of the bat hitting the ball. The crowd jumped up from their seats whistling and cheering. Baseball caps were tossed in the air. Kids slapped their hands together in high fives. Mikey, the team's MVP, had done it again. The bases were loaded, and Mikey hit another grand slam! Dad, beaming with pride, was hollering, "Atta boy, Mikey!"

Mikey was a good ballplayer, but he was not the team's most valuable player. Matter of fact, he never even made it to the all-stars, and the story I just told is not what really happened, but if I told you that story five years ago, I would have sworn he hit a grand slam and that Mikey was definitely the team's most valuable player. Five years ago, after Mikey died, I sat him on the throne at the same level as God, and I made him perfect: as perfect as our Heavenly Father. Not a good thing to do, but I did it anyhow.

The true story is that I had arrived at the ball field in just enough time to hear all the chanting. Mikey had hit the ball and made it to second base. The next batter stepped up to the plate, and Mikey was hunched over in a running position with one hand on his knee. He secretly tried to adjust his cup with his free hand, tugged on the bill of his ball cap, then raised his arm to the sky. I parked my butt in the chair that my husband faithfully brought to each game for me and grabbed the bag of sunflower seeds. It was late afternoon, and the brightness of the sun was blinding my view. Cupping my hand above my eyes, I leaned forward, squinting, and noticed that Mikey was holding up two fingers. I asked Bud, "What in the world is he doing?" Dad grinned and said that Mikey was letting him know that he just earned two bucks. Questioning my husband, I learned that Mikey and Dad had a secret pact. Mikey would get a dollar every time he got to first base, two dollars when he made it to second base, and five buckaroos when he hit a homerun. I was afraid to ask what he'd get for a grand slam.

Mikey earned a fair share of money during the baseball seasons. He wasn't an MVP, but he was a decent player and, more importantly, he had an attitude that was appealing to those around him. If teammates struck out, he would pat them on the back and tell them, "Good try." Win or lose, he left the field smiling. His sweet spirit was not left unnoticed, and he had left his mark in the hearts of all his coaches.

Mikey loved baseball. The San Francisco Giants were his favorite team, and Will Clarke was his main man. Jackie Robinson was his all-time hero. He looked forward to the day he would be "big" enough to play ball, and when that day finally came, his dad and I were the first ones in line to sign Mikey up for tee-ball. His first team was the Padres. The year was 1990, and Mikey was six years old. Every day, Mikey would dress in full uniform and parade around in anticipation of the games to begin. When opening day of baseball season finally arrived, Mikey was covered from head to toe with chicken pox. Though he was no longer contagious, his face was covered with the ugly sores, so we thought it was best that he did not participate in the opening-day festivities. Instead, we had him put on his uniform, cap and all, and he watched the parade from the car. We felt so badly for the little guy. He had looked forward to opening day for so long. I can still picture him all decked out in his uniform and brand-new cleats. With his baseball cap cocked to the side, he gazed out of the car window and watched as the kids marched by. Every so often he'd see a friend and smile a toothless smile, but I could tell that he had a heavy heart. His eyes were the windows to his soul and reflected his true feelings no matter how hard he tried to disguise them.

Later in the season, on Easter Sunday, Mikey broke his arm. For six weeks, Mikey dressed up in his uniform and sat on the sidelines, next to his dad, and watched his teammates. Attending the games and cheering for his teammates was Mikey's choice. That was the year he gained respect in the baseball community for his attitude. It was also the year Mikey would earn the nickname "Will." He truly believed he was a Will Clarke in the making. At the end-of-the-season party, his coach presented Mikey with a trophy that had "Will" engraved under his name.

My husband was a busy man and worked a lot of hours, but he always tried to make it to Mikey's games. There were only a few that he missed. During the week, it was hectic, but Bud rarely complained. He loved to watch Mikey play ball. Bud was the first to get off work so he could pick the boys up from daycare, rush home, give our sons a snack, and then head for the ball field. Dinner always had to wait until after the game, and usually all the snack-shack munching we did to kill the hunger pains while at the game spoiled our appetites. When Mikey started playing on the "farm team," the games were longer, and our dinners would be later. It was much too late to cook a meal, so we would stop for fast food after the games. During baseball season, we ate a lot of hamburgers, tacos, and pizza—a whole lot of pizza!

Mikey played baseball for eight years and then quit. He played one year on the "majors" and decided that he had had enough, and that was the beginning of the end of his baseball career. He never really talked about why he didn't want to play ball anymore, but I had my feelings as to why. His father had a massive stroke and became disabled the year Mikey entered eighth grade. Bud had a lot of physical problems, and sitting for two hours at a game was out of the question. I truly believe that Mikey did not want to play ball knowing that his dad would not be sitting on the sidelines. It would have been much too painful for Mikey not to hear his dad hollering, "Atta boy, Mikey!"

Mikey was twelve years old when his dad had the stroke. Although he was doing well in school, he had a difficult time at home adjusting to how the family dynamics had changed. He didn't have a problem helping me with his dad. Matter of fact, Mikey was interested in medicine and took the time to read about strokes so he would know how to care for him. He learned what to expect and was delighted in any ounce of progress his dad made. The problem occurred when he was told that his dad was in total charge all day, every day. Since Dad was at home all the time, Mikey was told not to call me at work unless it was an emergency. He was to go to his dad for all his needs and wants. That was scary for Mikey because I was always the one that was in charge and made the decisions until Dad got home from work. I was the easy parent who would give a reason for my no answers. Dad, being retired military, was strict; and when he said no, he meant no. When asked "why not?" he simply said, "Because I'm your father and I said no."

I'll always remember the day Mikey snuck and called me at work to ask if he could go to his friend's house.

"Hi, Mom, what are you doing?"

"I'm working, what are you doing?"

"Talking to you."

Then there was total silence.

"Mikey, what do you need?"

"Well, . . . I was wondering if I could go to Mansfield's house."

"Mikey, you know the rules. Your dad is home now, so you need to ask him."

The only reply I got was his heavy breathing on the other end of the phone.

"Mikey, did you ask your dad?"

"Yes."

"What did he say?"

"He said no!"

"So why are you calling me? If Dad said no, then he means no."

"I don't understand why I can't go to Mansfield's."

"Did you ask your dad why?"

"Yes."

Nothing but heavy breathing again.

"So . . . what did he say?"

"He said, 'Because I said no.' I told him I could walk to his house, but he said that I wasn't allowed to cross Highway 4."

"Well, Dad's right. Highway 4 is dangerous."

"It's not fair!"

"Mikey, I have work to do. I don't have time for this. We will talk when I get home."

I ended our conversation only to get another phone call a few minutes later.

"Hi, Mom, what are you doing?"

"I'm trying to work, Mikey. What do you think I'm doing?!"

Silence again.

"Mikey, what do you need now?"

"Well, . . . I thought that if I took the bus to Brentwood and not get off, it would bring me back to Oakley and I would be on the other side of the freeway."

"Sounds like a plan to me, but you still need to ask your dad."

"I did and he said no."

"Did he say why?"

"He said, 'Because I said so.'"

"There's your answer. Don't call me about this again!"

The conversation ended, and a few minutes later, my phone rang again.

"Mom, I'm sorry to bother you. I just wanted to tell you that I think it's time you start wearing the pants in this family again!"

I could not believe what I heard come out of Mikey's mouth. I literally had to cover my mouth with my hand to keep from screaming or possibly laughing. I knew what he said was inappropriate, and it ticked me off that he had the audacity to even make a comment like that, but I was also humored. Once I composed myself, I told Mikey that I had to go and that we would definitely talk about it later.

When I got home, Mikey was sulking in his room. He was still upset so I left him alone so that he could continue to have his little pity party. Later that evening, I went into his room, told him to move over, and crawled into bed with him. We had our talk, and he eventually apologized for his behavior and rude remark. That conversation was to mark only one of the many conversations that would follow in the years to come.

When Mikey entered high school, he still had no desire to become actively involved in any sports. As a freshman, he was the little man on campus, and his innocence was definitely noticeable. A lot of physical and emotional changes are taking place, and he seemed to be having a hard time trying to find himself. The first few months were difficult for him and I started to get concerned, but my husband reassured me that eventually Mikey would find his niche. All he needed was time to adjust. Bud was right. All Mikey needed was time, and within a few months, his social life begin to flourish and he gained back his self-esteem and confidence.

He began to spend more time with Joel, who had been his best friend since sixth grade. He also began dating Rosy. She was the turning point in Mikey's life. I began to see "524" written on everything and was later to learn that on May 24, Mikey and Rosy officially became an item. Instead of rushing to a sports game, I began to share the duties with Rosy's mom, Maria, carting the two to restaurants, movies, the bowling alley, and school dances. We spent a lot of time at the mall and took frequent trips to the ocean. On holidays, Mikey would spend half of the day with us and the other half with Rosy and her huge family. I didn't mind sharing Mikey on holidays. I grew up in a large family and wanted Mikey to experience what it was like to celebrate holidays in large gatherings. I also wanted him to be happy. We were always invited, but Bud was still recovering from his stroke and had become somewhat of a recluse. This saddened Mikey because he thought his dad was the biggest, strongest, most intelligent man that walked this earth. He did not like seeing him in such a vulnerable state. It all worked out because we ate our holiday meal early and Rosy's family ate in the late afternoon.

The summer after his freshman year, Mikey decided to play high school baseball. He signed up for the summer camp thinking it would ease him back into ball since he hadn't played for two years. I wasn't going to share the story about his stint with the team because it was just what I said—a stint! But it's a cute story, and it speaks to the heart of who Mikey was. Mikey had been away from baseball way too long, and it was a disastrous venture for him. The kid never got a hit, and while I was feeling sorry for him, he was laughing. "Mom," he said while laughing, "they throw the ball so fast I can't even see it!"

Mikey was also one of the youngest on the team. He was still innocent and somewhat naive, but he knew right from wrong. His dad was a good example of how gentlemen should behave, and as a result, Mikey grew to be a fine young man who did not like "locker room" talk. One day, on the way home from a game, Mikey had me cracking up.

"Mom."

"Yeah, Mikey."

"What's a continuation school?"

"I don't know. I think it's a special school for kids who can't get along well in a regular school."

"Uh-oh!"

"What?"

"Some kid from the other team asked me if our school was a continuation school."

"What did you tell him?"

"I just shrugged my shoulders and said that I thought it was."

"Get out of here! What did the kids say?"

"He said, 'Wow, this is a pretty nice continuation school.'"

We cracked up laughing because the high school is concrete, and with all the "locker room" talk, that is probably why the kid thought it was a continuation school. Needless to say, Mikey did not sign up for baseball again, but he did sign up for JV football. This really took my husband and me by surprise because Mikey did not know a thing about football.

Mikey and Rosy were still an item, and they looked cute together. Rosy in her cheerleading outfit and Mikey in his football uniform were the perfect picture of the "all-American couple." It's a good thing Mikey looked great in his uniform because for the first half of the season, the only playing he got to do was during practice. Mikey had a positive attitude and didn't seem to mind, but it was killing me. I felt sorry that he was not playing in the actual games.

Football turned out to be a good thing for our family. Although my husband was still not going out much, he had recovered quite a bit and attempted to go to the games. Once again, Bud loved watching

Mikey, and he was proud of our son even if he was always warming up the sidelines. He was proud of Mikey's attitude. Mikey was to reap the rewards during the second half of the season when the coach began playing him in the last few minutes of the game. Before long, he was given more playing time, and I was screaming a lot from the bleachers. Once, Mikey got a red (or was it yellow?) flag, and I jumped up and down, hollering and whooping because I just knew he did something great. My husband very calmly said, "Mom, sit down. Mikey just fouled!" Oops! After that embarrassing moment, I only hollered when everyone else did. Like the time Mikey sacked the quarterback. The crowd went nuts, and Dad was hollering, "Atta boy, Mikey!" I had no clue what he had done, but I knew it was something great, so I yelled with everyone else. Maybe even a little louder than the others. Later that evening, after Dad went home, Mikey and I were watching the varsity team when he asked me if I saw what he had done.

"Of course, I did. Didn't you hear me yelling?"

"Not really, all the voices blend together, and you can't distinguish one from another one on the field."

"Oh well, I yelled so loud I thought I was going to have to go fetch my tonsils off the field!"

"Mom, do you even know what I did?" He noticed that blank expression on my face. "Mom, do you know what a sack is?"

"Well, isn't that the thing that you put on your doohickey to keep it from getting hurt?"

Shall I say more? That night, my little man made his dad even more proud, taught me a little about football, and finished out the season playing instead of standing on the sidelines. On November 16, 1999, Mikey was honored with an award for his powerful performance as a defense lineman on the Freedom High School gridiron.

Although Mikey turned out to be a pretty good football player, one year was enough for him. It wasn't a sport that he enjoyed playing. He found it more exciting sitting in the bleachers hanging out with his friends and cheering for his school. I'll always remember the homecoming game just a few weeks before he died. He was a senior and dating a lovely girl named Stephanie because he and Rosy had broken up just four months earlier. I was on my way to work in the high school's snack shack when I heard him shout out to me. I looked up into the bleachers and just about died when I saw him. It was freezing that night, and there he was out in the cold, without a shirt, and painted in the school colors. He came down from the bleachers to give his momma a big kiss right there in front of all his friends, and he had a grin from ear to ear. His face, arms, chest, and back were painted purple and blue. He had a big *D* with a picture of a fence painted across his chest. I couldn't help but scream out with laughter. Mikey's character was remembered, after his death, by the senior class, and he was voted as the kid with the most school spirit.

Mikey discovered tennis in his junior year and loved it. That is another reason why he no longer had the desire to play football. He had a lot of respect for Coach Amaro, who made tennis even more inviting. Joel was playing tennis too, and they became doubles partners. Mikey and Joel were goofballs, and the two of them brought much laughter to their teammates at practices. During the games, I hear they were serious, but their easygoing nature and great attitudes were reflected in the high fives they slapped even when they lost a match. I stayed away from the games for two reasons. One, their games always started when I was still at work, and two, I am not sure Mikey wanted me there. He knew I had a big mouth and was fearful that I would cheer "loudly." However, he did invite me to the end-of-the-season tournament, and of course, I went. It was a Saturday, and when I got there, I noticed that Mikey appeared to be in some kind of pain. He kept reaching in his pocket and then rubbing something in his mouth. Brenda, Joel's mom, informed me that the tennis ball had hit him in his mouth the day before. It appeared to have loosened a tooth, which had begun to ache. He was trying to numb the pain with Anbesol. Mikey did not want to tell me because he was afraid I would pull him out of the tournament to take him to the dentist. When the tournament was over, I noticed that Mikey's face had started to swell. I knew we would be calling the dentist first thing Monday morning, but by evening, his face had blown up like a balloon. Two trips to the emergency room, a trip to the dentist, and two root canals later, Mikey's tooth was saved. I guess the pain was worth bearing because at the end of the season, Mikey won the Coaches Award for double partners.

Coach Amaro, who is also the athletic director and an English teacher, holds a tennis camp in June every year. It is a camp that draws in kids of all ages who have the desire to learn how to play tennis or enhance their skills. It is a great camp that prepares kids who are about to enter high school, join the tennis team, and compete in matches. Our neighbor, Jacob, signed up for three weeks of tennis camp. I went to watch him, and as he jumped around the court, I thought about Mikey and remembered the nickname his dad had given him. Before I reveal the nickname, I feel the need to explain that Mikey had danced a lot with Rosy and had been active in and taught gymnastics. Whenever Mikey returned from school, work, or wherever, his dad would always say, "Here comes Twinkle Toes!" Mikey would just smile because he knew it was his dad's pet name for him.

Tennis was a sport that Mikey truly enjoyed, and he was blessed to have a good coach that he looked up to. Not only did Mikey like Coach Amaro, but he truly loved and admired him too. Mikey often shared his feelings about Coach Amaro, and I can't help but think that Coach Amaro was more than just a coach. I do believe that he had become Mikey's mentor. Through the years, I came to know him, and I must agree with Mikey, Coach Amaro is a good example of a fine human being who gives his all to the students of Freedom High School.

Today, many tennis seasons after the accident, Joel and Mikey's memory lives on in the hearts of their coach, Steve Amaro. Their memory lives on in the hearts of the tennis players who knew the boys and in the hearts of tennis players who never knew them but have heard their story. Every year, the boys' tennis season starts with a tournament that has been renamed in honor of Joel and Mikey. It is called the Richards/Kelly Tennis Tournament.

As I lay in bed with my head under the covers, I silently wept a river of tears that soaked my pillow. I wasn't crying for myself. I was crying for a man whose rough and tough appearance was only a mask to protect his gentle heart. I was crying for a man whose little boy grew up to be a fine young man who made a difference in the world. A man whose son touched many lives because of the character he helped to build. I was crying for a man who was proud of his son and whose loss is just as horrific as mine. I was crying for my husband.

*For He has rescued us from the dominion of darkness
And brought us into the kingdom of the son He loves,
In whom we have redemption, the forgiveness of sin.*
—Colossians 1:13–14

Secrets Of The Heart

It was April 2005, just two weeks before Mother's Day. The church service had just ended when I heard someone softly calling my name.

"Mrs. Kelly," she called.

I turned to find a sweet young lady standing before me.

"Mrs. Kelly," she said, "I just wanted to tell you that Mikey was a kind person."

Pastor Reynolds had just preached on kindness, and it brought joy to my heart knowing that my son was remembered as a kind person.

"Ooooh, thank you," I replied. I reached to give her a hug when she began to speak again.

"I was in leadership class with Mikey, and we were both on the publicity committee together."

Her voice was soft, and her gentle words seemed to quiver as she spoke.

"I got pregnant and had a difficult time at school," she shared.

Her eyes sparkled from moisture as the tears threatened to fall.

"Mikey helped me through it," she said. "He . . . he was so kind."

I was touched by her words, and deep warmth spread through my body. I felt my heart flutter. It had been three and a half years since Mikey died. What a wonderful feeling knowing that my son was still remembered.

"I don't know why it took me so long to come to you." She placed her hand over her heart. "The Holy Spirit spoke to me when Pastor was talking about kindness, and I thought of Mikey. I'm sorry it took me so long."

I reached out and gave her a hug. I could feel her trembling.

"Honey, if you shared this with me when the accident happened, then what would I have to hear today? Everything is in God's timing."

I cried that afternoon. Big bittersweet tears. I cried because I missed my son. I cried because it brought joy to my heart knowing that he hadn't been forgotten, and I cried because I was ashamed. Ashamed because I had a story to tell and was too embarrassed to share it with the world. A secret locked in my heart for thirty-two years. A secret that needed to be revealed because it is part of my testimony. It has taken almost sixteen months to gather the strength and trust in God to give me the collection of words that will touch hearts and minister to you, my reader. I place my heart in your hands, and you can run anywhere you want with it. Just remember, Jesus lives in my heart and wherever you take it, He goes too.

This is my story.

Growing up in Maryland, I had the opportunity to experience the four seasons to their fullest. Although I am a summer person in spirit, the first heavy snowfall always enchanted me. Especially if the snow made its appearance in the early morning hours just before sunrise. The snow would still be soft and fluffy, not frozen by the chill of the evening or slushy from the warmth of the new day's sun. I'd look out of my window, through the eyes of a preteen, and see a blanket of snow creating the illusion of a winter wonderland. Bundled in warm clothes, an Ali MacGraw knitted hat, and a pair of galoshes, I'd go outside and head for the woods where the pureness of the snow was not yet tainted. I marveled at the beauty of the little tracks of footprints left by the snowbirds and hoped to catch a glimpse of them. I never saw one and assumed they were roosting nearby, snuggled in the snow, protecting them from the cold. I walked carefully and as quietly as I could so I wouldn't scare them and disturb their peace. I stayed in the woods until the warm rays of sunshine would sneak its way through the trees and begin the sun's melting process. I loved the crackling sound of the snow when it would slip and tumble from the branches. There in the quiet snow-covered woods, I never felt lonely because I always had a song in my heart.

In my teens, I got busy—really busy. I ditched the Ali MacGraw knitted hats and red galoshes for bell-bottom hip-huggers, bodysuits, string bikinis, and floppy hats. I liked being at school but hated doing the work. I was on the school gymnastics team, enjoyed playing tennis, and was an avid bike rider. My nieces and nephews were the light of my life. I fell in love with the ocean. I had a lot of girlfriends and dated little. I was a good kid making good choices until the world got ahold of me. I drifted from some of my closest friends, started going to parties, and smoked a little pot. I hated the taste of alcohol but drank it anyway. I wanted to belong, and amid all that mess, I really believed that I was having fun. Somewhere, somehow, I lost the song in my heart. I became lonely no matter who I was with, how many people were around, or how loud I laughed. There was a void in my heart that I couldn't seem to fill. When I was alone, I would often think of the snowbirds and I'd wonder, what happened to the little girl with the song in her heart?

When I was a senior in high school, I got my first job working in an old-fashioned ice cream parlor, earning sixty-five cents per hour. It was a fun job, and after graduation, I began to work a lot of hours. Most of the customers were midshipmen from the US Naval Academy, located in Annapolis, Maryland, and in June, we would be swamped with their families and girlfriends who would come from all over the United States for the June week festivities and graduation. I met a midshipman and fell in love that year. Or at least the kind of love that an eighteen-year-old thinks is love. We dated for the summer of 1972 and into the spring of the following year. I settled down and went to the community college to fulfill a forgotten dream. With aspirations of becoming a gym teacher, I studied during the week and dated my Middy on the weekends. Life was good—for a while. In early spring, I found myself in trouble and made a choice that an eighteen-year-old should not make alone. I did not confide to my mom because I was so ashamed. In April 1973, my Middy and I went to Washington DC to take care of the "situation" and make it all go away.

I cried uncontrollably as I lay shivering on the cold mattress that crinkled each time I moved. I was so ashamed, and the emotional pain of what I was doing hurt more than words could say.

"Come on now, it's not that bad. Settle down!" the nurse scolded.

She was dressed in white. Everything was white. The walls, the linens, even the doctor was clothed in white. White, cold, and sterile. The only colors in the room were the silver stirrups that my feet were in and the instruments that the doctor was using to perform the "procedure."

"This is a simple procedure," the doctor said. "If you calm down, it won't take long. I'm going to give you a little something to relax you." His tone was as cold as the room, with not an ounce of compassion. I felt the prick from the injection and began to feel the effects of the drug. Everything became fuzzy, and the voices I heard seemed to be coming from far away. I closed my eyes and began floating . . . floating back to a place that brought me comfort. Floating to a place that was also white, but exceedingly beautiful. I drifted to the quiet of my winter wonderland with the snow-covered trees, where my beloved snowbirds were hidden from their predators as they snuggled in the snow to keep warm. My soul was temporarily at peace.

"Ms. Ritter," she whispered. "Ms. Ritter, you can get dressed and go now."

When I opened my eyes, I noticed that I was in a different room. For a brief moment, I was disoriented. The lady in the room was gentle spoken and seemed very kind. As I was leaving, she told me that if I followed the recovery directions on my discharge papers, everything would be all right. Then she told me that no one will ever know what I did. She said it was my secret.

Within two weeks, I got a horrendous fever and acquired an infection that racked my body. I was hospitalized for almost a week. Final diagnosis: pelvic inflammatory disease. One morning, I woke up to find my mother softly crying at my bedside. I don't know what the doctor had told her. She never confronted me, and I never asked. She just cried.

I never saw my Middy again. We went our separate ways. I dropped out of college, and as time passed, I continued to work at various jobs. I tried to forget about the secret I carried in my heart. When I was twenty-one, I met a man seventeen years older than me. He became my friend and confidante. Our friendship blossomed, and before I knew what hit me, I was in love. He was a Seabee in the US Navy, and when he got a new set of orders to the Philippines, I was devastated. He wanted to marry me but thought it best that we waited for a year to make sure it was what I wanted. He was concerned about our age difference but promised to send for me in a year's time if I still wanted to marry him. Within three months, I knew he was my soul mate, and with my mother's well wishes, I bought a ticket, packed my bags, and flew to the Philippines to be with him. Within a year's time, we were married; and before long, I wanted to have his baby. I wanted to have my very own family.

Instead of a baby, my chronic inflammatory disease returned, causing severe complications. The navy doctor recommended a hysterectomy. He said it was my only cure. I was heartbroken, but my beloved husband, always the joy giver, said we could adopt. Matter of fact, we had intentions to adopt a child from the Philippines, but I never learned to speak Tagalog fluently. We had concerns about communication issues.

In the early hour of a Friday morning, my husband took me to the hospital where I was admitted and prepped for surgery. I was given a shot to relax me and was taken to OR. Next thing I knew, the doctor was telling me that the surgery was cancelled because the instruments he needed to use were not sterile enough to his satisfaction. The surgery was rescheduled for the following Monday. He said I would be given a "chit" for the weekend and be released as soon as the anesthesia wore off. A "chit" is a military term for pass. I was sent to a room with a lady that just had surgery, and she was crying hysterically. She was screaming out in pain. I got scared and became upset. My husband decided to take me out of the hospital immediately, which was not an easy task, but he managed to have me discharged quickly. We chose to go to Clark Air Force Base to see a different doctor for a second opinion. Once again, surgery was scheduled except this time it was for exploratory surgery to access my condition. What a blessing that doctor was. He said I did not need a hysterectomy and gave me antibiotics. He advised me to wait until we returned to the States before any more decisions were made. He recommended I see an infertility specialist. That doctor gave me hope.

In 1978, we returned to the States with orders to Concord Naval Weapons Station in California. For our first year, we lived in town in a rented home. My pelvic disease seemed to disappear, so I tried to have a baby again, but it just wasn't happening. I decided to go to work instead. Eventually, we moved on base and had the privilege of living in officer housing. Life was good, but I began to yearn for a baby again. I went to Oak Knoll Naval Hospital and received treatment by two wonderful infertility doctors who ran a battery of tests and confirmed that I had only 2 percent chance of ever having children. I was heartbroken. Although I still felt shame, I was honest with the doctors and revealed that I had had an abortion. The surgeons saw my pain, and without any promises, they gave me a little hope by agreeing to perform plastic surgery on my fallopian tubes. This was a procedure that could take up to five hours. They told me that once they opened me up, the surgery would only be performed if there was a 10 percent or better chance of getting pregnant. I had the surgery in January 1980 and woke up to a navy chaplain praying over me. I honestly thought I had died and gone to heaven. I'd never had anyone pray over me before. When I realized I was still alive, I slowly reached down and softly touched my abdomen. To my great delight, I felt this great big bandage and knew the surgery was performed. I knew that I had at least 10 percent chance of having a baby. That sure beat the odds I originally had been given. You can imagine my delight when I was to learn following the surgery that my chances had increased to 40 percent. I don't remember thanking God.

In July 1980, the song in my heart returned. I was going to have my own little family. April 1981, I gave birth to the most beautiful baby boy. I named him Bernard Lee Kelly III. We call him Buddy. I proudly named him after the most wonderful man I know—my soul mate, my husband. Two years, eight months, and seventeen days later, I gave birth to another beautiful baby boy. Michael Patrick Kelly entered this world in January 1984. We called him Mikey. My own little family was complete, and I was blessed beyond anything that can be measured. My miracle sons, the lights of my life. My most precious treasures. My little snowbirds in a winter wonderland. I don't remember thanking God.

I finally had my very own little family, and I was on top of the mountain. I loved being a mother and had this crazy, delusional notion that I was going to be the best mom ever. Although I had to work, my sons were always my top priority. My husband and I selected the best daycare providers we could find. When my children were not feeling well, I stayed home. When I wasn't feeling well, my children stayed home. I loved being with them and couldn't stand sending them off to daycare when I was home. They made me feel better. I read to them every evening no matter how tired I was. All three of us would crawl into one bed and read a story. Then I'd let each son pick out a book, and I'd spend individual time with them in their own rooms.

We went to the park often and spent a great deal of time at the ocean. We went fishing and took a lot of spontaneous road trips exploring Northern California. As the years passed and the boys started school, I always took time off work to attend school conferences, field trips, and awards ceremonies. My vacation time was spent helping in the classrooms. I was being the perfect mom in my storybook family.

I just painted a nice picture of myself as a mom, didn't I? Trust me, I told the truth. What I did not tell you was that I had quite a temper. When things got a little hairy, I would scream, yell, holler, and sometimes spank, but mostly threatened and eventually, give in. Not a good way to handle things, but I did it that way. My poor sons would look at me as though I was some kind of crazy lady. I'd explode and two minutes later I would be fine and wonder why everyone was mad at me. We had our good times and not-so-good times, but through it all, my family was and is the joy of my life. They give me reason to live.

The November 20, 2001, tragedy shattered our family into itty-bitty pieces. You know the story. A horrific car accident took the life of one of my little snowbirds. My Mikey was taken from me in the blink of an eye. My little angel on earth was taken home to be with our Heavenly Father. My precious son who never really belonged to me. He was just a gift for me to take care of for a little while. A special gift that was put on this earth for a purpose and, once the purpose was fulfilled, taken home to be with the Lord.

Lord, I know that my Mikey is in your presence now and he is seeing the face of Jesus. Although I wanted more time with my son, I am so grateful for the seventeen years I had with him. He was one of my miracle babies that I almost never had. I cannot imagine never having known his sweet soul. Thank you, Lord, for choosing me to be his earthly mother and trusting me to care for him. Thank you for always being with me, even when I didn't know you were. Thank you for all the days of my life. For the good days and bad days, for the sad days and the happy days. And, Lord, although I never asked for them, I need to thank you for all the tragedies that you allowed to come my way. I now understand that the good tears and the bad tears need to blend together to make me who I am today. I ask that you continue to do your work in me so that I can continue to grow in you. Thank You, Lord, for Sarah. She is a courageous young lady. Her courage gave me courage to share my story, so people can understand why I am thankful for the short time I had with Mikey. I will be full of sorrow all of my remaining days on earth, but I know you understand. You know the pain I am in, and you are pleased with me for loving so deeply. Most of all, I thank you, Lord, for your forgiveness. Because of your forgiveness and redemption, I have been set free.

He makes me lie down in green pastures, He leads me beside still waters, He restores my soul.
—Psalms 23:2–3

The Chicken Walk

According to the church guestbook, more than six hundred of Mikey's friends, family, and others that he had touched gathered as Mikey was laid to rest. Friends tell me that the sky was bright blue with big white puffy clouds, left over from the heavy rains we had two days before. The sun was shining, but I was told that the afternoon air was cold and crisp. Falling leaves gently dropped from the trees and were tossed around by the slight breeze that signified winter was near. I didn't see the blue sky and the white clouds, nor did I see the falling leaves. The rays of sun did not bring me warmth. My world was dark that November day. Through my eyes, I saw a hazy sky full of stormy clouds that were tinted gray. I felt the crisp air, but was too numb to feel its coldness.

Bagpipers played sweet sounds of "Amazing Grace" as the pallbearers gently carried Mikey to his grave site. A spray of long-stemmed red roses covered his casket like a blanket. His surfboard was propped up against a crape myrtle tree. A personal touch from our neighbor, Mark, in remembrance of Mikey's passion for surfing. Although I sat just a few feet from Mikey's casket, I could hardly look at it. I could not bear the thought of my precious baby being locked in that "box." It was too painful and much too final. As the service began, I heard the familiar voice of my pastor, Rev. Dennis Reynolds, but I did not hear his words. I was consumed with grief. My body was present, but my mind was absent. I missed my son. I wanted my Mikey back.

We buried Mikey in an area that is located near a fence with oleander bushes alongside it. There are many old oak trees scattered throughout the cemetery. The land is flat, and the grass is green and well kept. In the distance, you can see Mount Diablo, a place we frequently visited while my sons were growing up. I go to the cemetery often.

There are usually a lot of birds chirping and fluttering in the trees or frolicking around in the bushes. Occasionally, I've seen squirrels chasing one another, and wild cats roam freely. I have become familiar with the noises that the critters make there. The cemetery is a peaceful place. There, in my quiet moments, I am able to talk to Jesus and pray without any interruptions.

One Saturday afternoon, fourteen months after Mikey died, I went to the cemetery to clean Mikey's memorial plaque and arrange fresh flowers in his vase. Mikey's birthday had just passed. He would have been nineteen years old. I was in a weepy state of mind, and for the first time since his death, I threw a little pity party. Yes, that's right—a pity party. No guests, just me and my "Why, God? Why my son? We had dreams! We had our future all planned out! Why, God? Why did you take away my joy?" I was deep in thought, wallowing in self-pity, when all of a sudden, I heard a rustling noise in the bushes. The dry leaves made such a loud crackling sound that it startled me. When I looked up, I could not believe what I saw. There before me was a chicken! He came strutting through the bushes bebopping his way toward me.

There are no words that can express the emotions that flip-flopped at that moment. The pity and grief were washed away, and I began to laugh softly from deep within my soul. I felt as though the chicken was dancing just for me. It was then that "the Chicken Walk" memory came back to me and filled me with pure joy. With tears streaming down my face, I stayed and watched that chicken for quite some time and just reflected.

Mikey was quite a character. Although he had a serious side to his nature, he loved to "act out" with me. I don't know why, but when we went to this one particular supermarket, we would do what we called "the Chicken Walk." Not once did we do this at any other store. Our performance was usually in the parking lot. It was spontaneous, never planned. Mikey would squat low to the ground and swing his long legs around and strut like a chicken. He'd be strutting and bebopping around, grinning from ear to ear. I would stoop as low as this ol' body would let me, strut, bob my neck, and flutter my arms. Some days we would get bold and cluck like a chicken. We loved the reactions we got from people. Some would laugh, and others would look at us as if to say, "Whatchu been smoken'?" I used to tell Mikey that we didn't need drugs because we were naturally high. Mom and son, totally enjoying each other's company. High on life, experiencing genuine happiness. We would get into our truck laughing so hard that there would be tears in our eyes. In the midst of the laughter, Mikey would look at me and say, "You're crazy." I would reply by saying, "Yea, I know and guess what? I'm your momma!" Our hearts would burst with joy.

I don't believe in "chance" happenings. The sudden appearance of that chicken was a profound, personal message. It represented intimate moments that Mikey and I shared. Only God knew what joy that chicken would bring. Only God knew how much I needed that chicken at that moment.

I have come to understand that those of us sitting on the "mourning bench" hold sole ownership of our grief. Each of us walk through the valley of death in our own unique way, and as we journey through the different phases of bereavement, we have the freedom to sit on our bench for as long as it takes to catch our breath. The journey is long and tiresome. There will be times when it will feel like a never-ending roller coaster ride, with one's emotions taking sudden twists and turns. Almost getting through the day without shedding tears, then seeing something as trivial as a favorite snack can turn one into melted snow, leaving one standing in a puddle of tears. I hear this is part of the grieving process and that I need to go through all the phases in order to heal, but I have also come to realize that I need to be careful. Sometimes I get so swallowed up in grief and self-pity that I tend to forget the precious moments of joy that I had shared with Mikey.

The Bible says that we will receive rest. It does not say when or how the rest will come. It does not even promise how long the rest will last. The rest is just promised. In the midst of my sadness, God gave me rest. He restored my soul by tapping on my heart and reminding me about the chicken walk. I savor that memory and have stored it in my heart, never to forget again. Today, when grief and pity start to consume me, I turn my thoughts back to that moment, and I am able to softly cry with a warm smile on my face.

You too can receive the rest that God promises. Be still, wait on the Lord, and listen to your heart. When the rest comes, grab hold of it and know that it comes from our loving God.

But those that hope in the Lord
Will renew their strength
They will soar on wings like eagles
They will run and not grow
weary, They will walk and not
faint.

—Isaiah 40:31

Free-Fallen

"Mom."

"What?"

"I want to skydive."

"Sure, tomorrow."

"No, Mom, I'm serious. I really want to skydive."

Mikey had my attention. I could not believe what I was hearing come out of his mouth.

"Get out of here! Are you crazy?" I knew my son was a risk taker, but I thought he set boundaries. This, to me, was more than stepping over the line. It was suicidal.

"Why?"

"I don't know." He shrugged. "For the thrill, I guess."

"Are you out of your mind!"

"Maybe so, . . . but I'm going to do it."

"Go for it. But not until you're eighteen."

"Rosy's dad was going to take me when I turned eighteen. No chance of that happening since we aren't going together anymore."

"Well, don't look at me 'cause this is one thing I ain't gonna do with you."

"Yes, you will," he said with a big grin.

"No, I won't!"

"Yes, you will," he said with an even bigger grin.

I did.

It was June 2004 when I took the leap. Only my Mikey wasn't there to jump with me. He died just eight weeks shy of his eighteenth birthday, never having the opportunity to experience the thrill he so looked forward to. So I jumped for him and, more importantly, I jumped for me. I needed the closure.

Once I made the decision to skydive, I got excited when the day finally came. When my tandem partner was introduced to me as "Michael," I was ecstatic. Out of all the instructors there, I was given one with the name of Michael. Coincidence? I don't think so. I believe that God was sending me a message reminding me that my Mikey was with me in spirit. I could envision his silly grin and imagined that he was saying, "I knew you'd jump, Mom."

Yes, my son knew me well.

Before boarding the plane at the parachute center, Pastor Marc Anderson, his family, and I formed a circle; and with our hands joined together, we prayed. I believe in the power of prayer so when we boarded the small plane, I was relaxed, and the excitement continued to escalate. I goofed around and chatted with my tandem partner. When it was my turn to jump, I calmly listened to Michael as he briefed me on what I needed to do. I felt no fear until I was standing at the door. I looked down and saw the earth below me. Little squares and circles, in various sizes, creating the images of a map. Miles and miles of nothing but air between me and land. My heart began to pound, and I broke out into a cold sweat. My fingers and toes began to tingle, and for about two seconds, I felt nothing but extreme fear. I was sure that I was going to have a heart attack or wet my pants. Maybe both!

Plunging thirteen thousand feet from a small noisy airplane that was traveling just under 80 miles an hour, I put my life in God's hands and, to my surprise, I laughed. As I was free-falling at an accelerating speed of 125 miles per hour, I laughed. The surge of excitement was electrifying. I laughed and laughed, and yes, you guessed it, I laughed some more.

Then with my lips flapping from the force of the wind, I screamed out, "This is for you, Mikey!" Although I screamed it as loud as I could, no audible sound could be heard from my voice. I imagined that my voice was carried to heaven and heard by my son. Oh, what a glorious spring morning! The sky was a beautiful blue, and there was not a cloud in sight. What I remember most is the silence. Total silence void of all earthly sounds. Just me, my mind, and my heart screaming with joy. For sixty seconds, I was free. I was an eagle soaring through the sky with my wings spread wide, totally free! Free of all the pain and sorrow I had been inflicted with since Mikey's death. The weight of the cross I had been carrying no longer weighed heavily upon my shoulders. I was free!

The sixty-second free fall was not enough for me, and when Michael opened the chutes, I was quite disappointed. Especially since the sudden change of pace sent waves of nausea rumbling through my tummy as we drifted for the next four minutes. By the time we landed, I was disoriented and feeling slightly green but ready to do it again.

The free falling was a thrill like none I had ever experienced before.

When I look up into the sky and I see an airplane, I think of Mikey. I see a young man who never had the chance to fulfill a dream he once had, and I see me, a mom who had no desire to jump from a plane but did it anyways. I often ask myself why. Did I really take the leap to bring closure to an unfinished chapter of Mikey's life, or did I do it to fulfill one of Mikey's many dreams? What was my true motive?

I am blessed! I have a wonderful husband who told Mikey he was crazy for wanting to jump out of a perfectly good airplane and thought I was equally nuts, but he supported my decision. He knew the special bond that Mikey and I had, and it saddened him to see me suffer. Although for financial reasons I should not have done it, he never once balked at the expense. He went along with the "closure" thing, but deep inside, he knew that it would take me to another level of healing.

I am blessed! The day after Mikey died, I met his girlfriend's mom, Sandy, and we have been friends since. Matter of fact, she has become one of my best friends—always there when I need her. Sandy, Stephanie, and a puppy named Rusty were there to watch me and patiently listened to my chatter about the jump for hours afterward. I once read a phrase that stated, "Friends are the flowers in the garden of life." Not only is that a beautiful quote but a true one. Sandy is a flower in my garden. She listens endlessly to my stories of Mikey, some of which I am sure to have repeated many times because as time goes on, I have no new memories to share. Thank You, Lord, for the many flowers you have given me.

I am blessed and so is my family! In the midst of our storm, God has given us rest. Through my insanity, sunlight brightened the hearts of my husband and son, Buddy, as we watched my outrageous skydiving video. Laughter filled our family room, and joy filled our hearts. My family is the brightest of all flowers in my garden of life.

So I asked myself again, what was my true motive for skydiving? I honestly can say that I have no clue. I doubt that I will ever be able to comprehend the reasoning behind my insane adventure, but that's okay. It is the end result and how it helped me and my family that counts.

Oakie Olympics

Usually when new neighbors move in, I am the one peeking out the window to get a glimpse of them. Not that I am nosy. I just like to know how old they are and if they have kids. Okay, maybe I am a little bit nosy; but eventually, I do go over and introduce myself when I see them out in their yard. It wasn't like that when the Coopers moved in next door though. Mikey and Buddy were acting out and giving me a hard time. It must have been early morning because Mikey was in his room getting dressed when the arguing started. I don't remember how it escalated to the point when Mikey ran out the front door in his underwear, Buddy running behind him, and me chasing them with a spatula fussing and cussing, all the while my new neighbor taking it all in. Later, when we became friends, she said that she thought, "Lord, what kinda neighbors did we move next to?"

We all became pretty good friends. She had two sons around the same age as my boys, and they enjoyed hanging out together. Tip was the oldest son, and Aram a few years younger. Nice boys. It was a sad day when they moved out of the area several years later. We have kept in touch, and when they heard about Mikey's passing, the boys came to visit. The drive is a couple of hours so they have come to visit periodically though the years. During these visits, they have shared many stories that I have not heard before. The one I am about to share warms my heart and gives me so much joy every time I think about it. I just hope I can paint a picture to give you a visual of how funny it must have been. The boys called it Oakie Olympics.

Tip's friend lived on a farm out in the country. One day, he asked Aram and Mikey if they wanted to go to the farm with him. He wanted to visit with his friend and do some work while there. His friend's father had an old 1974 Chevy pickup that Tip really wanted. The father said he could have it, but he had to work it off. The pickup was brown in color that had been sideswiped so the driver's side was destroyed. I was told that it looked like a gardener's truck with cheap chrome wheels that were starting to show rust. It had a three-speed tranny with a granny gear. Tip must have seen potential in that old truck because I can't imagine why he wanted it.

It was a hot day in July, and I guess the boys became bored and got a harebrained idea to tie a wooden pallet to the back of the pickup and take a joyride. Two two-by-fours were nailed to the side of the pallet to use as rails, a piece of carpet was put on top of the pallet to sit on, and they tied a rope to the back of the truck to hold on to. There was no way to steer. Tip did most of the driving because he was the only one with a license, but they all took turns. They would haul butt down the long driveway, do donuts in the field, and then go back down the driveway. It was estimated that they were going about thirty miles per hour in second gear. They had to stop several times because the rope would break or cool off the radiator because it was shot and start to overheat. The field in front of the stables were dusty because it was mostly dirt with a little bit of grass. Snowboard goggles were used to keep the dust and dirt out of their eyes. I was told that Mikey was smiling and laughing so hard that the dust and dirt collected in his mouth and turned to mud. He had mud in between every tooth. I sure wish I had a picture! After about a half hour, the wooden pallet gave out and they went back to work where they were supposed to be hauling junk to the dump. It's a great memory that the boys (now married men with children of their own) still laugh about over twenty years later. It was a moment in time that Mikey never shared with me. I am sure it was because he knew I would have had a hissy fit. Someone could have tumbled off and broken their neck!

So many stories have been shared through the years. All have been stored in a special place in my heart. I love each and every story told.

Some memories have been tucked away and forgotten about, but they always seem to pop up just when I need to be lifted up. I am so grateful that God has surrounded me with family and friends that continue to reminisce about Mikey! I am blessed!

Carry each other's burdens,
And in this way
You will fulfill the law of Christ.

—Galatians 6:2

Graveyard Friends

In the still of the night when it seemed as though all the world was sleeping, I would be awake, the wood in the fireplace no longer flickering and crackling or bringing warmth to the room. The fire had long since burned out, leaving nothing left but a pile of ashes. Most of the time I'd lie on the couch, curled up in a little ball. Wrapped in a throw blanket, I tried to hide from the enemy that I knew would come soon. Satan, the enemy, always came in the wee hours of the morning to taunt me and feed me lies. I tried to lock him out, but he always managed to find a crack and sneak his way in to play havoc with my mind.

It was during those quiet moments when I thought I would go out of my mind, especially when it rained. I'd hear the wind blowing and the rain pelting against the house. No matter how hard I try to resist, the storm would beckon me to the window. Peering out into the darkness, I'd see the rain pouring from the sky drenching the ground and the trees swaying from the force of the wind. Tormented, I would cry for my Mikey. I cried because my baby was all alone in the cold, dark cemetery and he was being rained on. I wanted to go to him, but my spirit knew that what I was feeling was not of God. While the enemy was trying to lure me to the cemetery at that eerie hour, I'd hear God whispering that Mikey was not in the grave.

Early in the morning, when the sun had risen and the world awakened, I would go to the cemetery to visit Mikey's grave where his precious bones lay beneath the bed of red roses that his father had purchased. I'd kneel and thank Jesus for helping me through the night, and yes, I must admit, I talked to Mikey. At lunchtime, I'd go back to the grave and would find cards and letters that were addressed to our family. Often there would be letters to Mikey. The ones stapled shut remained closed, the writers' private words unread and left until the paper dissolved into the ground. Flowers, stuffed animals, tennis balls, and little trinkets would be left, signifying that his friends had come to visit. Sometimes I'd go to the grave and find Stephanie there grieving for Mikey, and it would break my heart. I'd embrace her and give her words of comfort but never tried to stop her tears. I knew that she needed to grieve in order to heal.

At dusk when all the world was gathering with their families to eat their dinner and settle in for the night, I'd be drawn back to the grave to say good night to Mikey. Then I'd go home and wait for the enemy because I knew he would come; he always did. In the still of the night when all was quiet. I'd put on my shield of armor and prepare for battle, a fierce battle that tormented my soul and exhausted me, but one that I always won because my Lord Jesus was there to carry me victoriously through the night. I know it sounds crazy, and you are probably wondering how I could have been so tormented and still claim victory. The victory came in the morning. Although I would awaken with a heavy heart and have no desire to face another day without Mikey, I was still breathing. I endured another night, and when the sun would rise, it never ceased to amaze me that I would wake up to find my heart still beating. Even with all that heart-wrenching pain that was so very raw, I continued to breathe.

I routinely went to Mikey's grave three times a day for two months. Rain or shine, I was there. During those months, I cried a lot and had a hard time believing that his precious bones lay beneath me. Wasn't it just moments ago when he too walked on this earth? His laughter was so fresh in my mind, and memories of days gone by flashed before my eyes like a picture show. How could it be possible that my vibrant son's bones could be buried six feet in the ground when he still seemed so alive to me?

In the beginning when I went to the cemetery, it was all about Mikey. While I mourned the loss of my son and all of his unfulfilled dreams, I was oblivious to my surroundings. I was so absorbed in my own pain that I didn't pay any attention to the other graves, much less the people that were visiting. Then one day, my husband came home from the cemetery and asked if I noticed all the new people that moved into Mikey's neighborhood. "Matter of fact," he announced, "Mikey has a new neighbor that just moved in." At first, I wasn't sure I heard him correctly. Mikey had a new neighbor? What the heck was he talking about? Then I realized what he was telling me, and I cracked up, laughing. I laughed because only he could face death for what it was in such a lighthearted way. Later, as I stood by the new grave at the foot of Mikey, I cried. I cried because my big teddy bear of a husband, who was in such horrific pain, was so selfless and he still took the time to acknowledge others that had passed away. I was to learn from the graveyard diggers that the person who took up residence in Mikey's neighborhood was a sixteen-year-old boy who died in a car accident. That was June of 2002.

The flowers from that sixteen-year-old boy's funeral soon wilted and were replaced with a strip of sod, which eventually grew and blended in with the other grass. As time passed, I began to wonder why he didn't have a marker, not even a temporary one. It bothered me because there were no visual signs that there was a grave there, so I began to share Mikey's flowers and would lay them on the grass. One afternoon while I was cleaning Mikey's plaque, I noticed some young people wandering around. They were carrying a small bouquet of roses, and I could hear them whisper that they were sure the grave was nearby. The oldest boy soon bent over and placed the roses on an empty patch of grass.

I stood up and gently asked, "Are you looking for the sixteen-year-old that died in June?"

"Yes, that's my brother," the older boy replied. "Did you know him?"

"No, I just know of him, and he is buried right here at the feet of my son."

They picked up the flowers and placed them where I knew the grave was and began talking to me. They shared stories about their little brother that made me laugh and cry. I was given the opportunity to share my faith and how Jesus was carrying me through my darkest moments, and before they left, each one of them gave me a hug and thanked me. As of this day, I have yet to see them again, but I often pray that the seed of hope was planted in their hearts that day.

I returned to work two months after Mikey died. Although I knew Mikey's true residence was in heaven with Jesus and that he was not in the grave, I continued to go to the cemetery every day after work and on weekends. I would clean his plaque and replace his flowers with fresh ones several times a week. I didn't think it was a proper way for a Christian woman to behave, but I went anyhow. It made me feel better.

As time passed, I no longer cried at the cemetery. It became a familiar place, and as much as I hate to say it, I became as comfortable in the cemetery, during the day, as I am in my own backyard. I started roaming around, visiting other grave sites; and when it was appropriate, I talked to others that were visiting a loved one. I met a lot of lovely people while wandering around, and I have heard many sad stories. I was to understand that most people come to the cross in their darkest moments. When they are hurting, there is a deep hunger for peace, and some call out to God for comfort, but still find no peace. It was during those moments that I have had the opportunity to share my faith and hope that I have because of what happened after the cross. It blows my mind to know that Jesus died on the cross to take away the sins of the entire world, but that is not where the Gospel of Christ ends. The most glorious moment of all is when He rose again, in three days, so that we can have eternal life. Eternal life in heaven where the broken are made whole again. A place where there is no longer any more pain or tears. A place where I envision green pastures filled with beautiful flowers with colors so brilliant only the spiritual eye can look at because the brightness would blind the human eye. A place where there are angels and no demons, and as you walk along the streets paved in gold, you have no fear for there is no war or gangs. You no longer hear gunshots or the sound of sirens. Instead, you hear beautiful music as the angels sing "Holy, Holy, Holy." There you see the face of Jesus as He wraps His arms around you and welcomes you home. I share how I have invited Jesus into my heart so that I can have peace within my soul while I wait until it is my turn to enter into His kingdom. The graveyard has become my mission field.

Some of my most touching stories come from the cemetery, extremely sad moments but so very powerful because the encounters could only have been orchestrated by God.

Thanksgiving Day 2002, just one year after Mikey died, has become one of those precious stories that will always be embedded in my heart. That day, I decided to go to the cemetery early. My intent was to visit with Mikey and go home to be with my living family where I belonged. When I got to the cemetery, I was thankful that none of my graveyard friends were there because I didn't want to take time to talk with them. I wanted to visit with Mikey and go home. It was cold and very foggy. I didn't notice the lone figure bent over a new grave until I was leaving. When I saw the figure, I stopped for a brief moment; and though I could not hear any crying, my spirit could feel that person's sorrow. I shrugged it off and told myself that I needed to go home and went to my car.

I put my key in the ignition, started the car, and was about to drive off when the Holy Spirit tugged at my heart. I looked in my rearview mirror, saw the lone figure, and cried out, "Ohhh, God, I don't have time for this. I need to get home!" I really wanted to leave, but I turned off the car and got out. As I approached, I noticed that the person was dressed all in black. The black beanie cap was pulled down so low that I could not tell if it was a man or a woman, boy or girl.

I stood there quietly. The sorrow was so thick in the air that I felt as though it were wrapping around me. I felt like I was intruding and wanted to quietly walk away, but it was too late. When the person looked up at me, I was speechless. There, looking up at me was a young woman whose big brown eyes were so full of pain that I knew without being told she was mourning the loss of a child. Grief distorted her face as a river of silent tears streamed down her cheeks.

For a moment, we just stared at each other then I gently asked, "Would you like a hug?" She nodded, stood up, and as she gently embraced me, I could feel her trembling. I asked no questions, but she shared and I was to learn that her son had died a violent death.

He was only eighteen years old. My hug did not and could not take away her pain, but I believe it gave her a brief moment of comfort. I went home that morning with a heavy heart, but so very grateful that my son did not die a violent death. He was not taken by the hands of someone else, and he did not suffer. I thanked God for His mercy that Thanksgiving Day.

I am not sure why, but I had a strong need to stop by the cemetery every day after work. During the winter months, it would be pitch-black out when I'd roll in around 5:30 p.m., and I have to admit that it was really spooky when no one else was there. I'd park my car, leave my headlights on, and run like the dickens to Mikey's grave. I'd stay long enough to check out his flowers, say "Hey, Mikey," then beat feet. One evening, I noticed that all the little trinkets that his friends had left were gone. I thought, "What the heck" then remembered the stories I had heard about the graveyard thieves. At first, I was ticked off because I never really expected it would happen to me. I don't know why I thought I would be exempt. I just did. I eventually shrugged it off, telling myself that whoever took the trinkets must have needed them more than Mikey. After all, they were only placed there for our own comfort.

The following weekend when I was putting fresh flowers in Mikey's vase, I felt the presence of someone standing behind me. I turned around and saw that it was one of the graveyard workers.

"I almost caught him," he said.

"Who?" I asked.

"The little thief that stole Mikey's stuff."

"You're kidding, who was it?" I asked.

"Some kid. Couldn't have been more than nine or ten years old," he replied.

"Probably lives in that housing development over there. When I saw him messing around the grave, I hopped in my golf cart and came over as fast as I could, but he got away."

"Thanks, but it's okay. Maybe the kid needed something to play with."

"Well, I doubt he'll be coming back anytime soon," he said.

"Oh yeah, why do you say that?"

"'Cause as he was running off, I hollered, 'I know where you live!'"

We laughed but I later thought about that poor boy. He probably didn't sleep all night for fear that the graveyard digger was going to come and get him.

My daily rituals to the cemetery continued for over two years and then they stopped. Coming home from work one evening, I started to turn into the cemetery but changed my mind and just drove by. You can call it healing if you want, but the plain truth is, I was tired. I was sick and tired of being tired, and I knew that the craziness had to come to an end. Even though I knew Mikey wasn't in the grave, I felt guilty so I did my drive-bys for a while and eventually that was to stop also, but I still went to the cemetery every weekend. To this day, I go to the cemetery every Sunday, after church, and place fresh flowers on Mikey's grave.

Time does not heal, but healing does come with time if you allow it to happen. It is a choice we all can make. It is a choice I am grateful that I made, and the true impact of that decision was to touch the depth of my soul several years later.

Our pastor loves to give us challenges. "Go out into the world and spread the gospel of Jesus Christ," he'd say. "Be a witness and touch someone's life." This particular Sunday, he challenged us to pray to God and ask him to bring someone into our path so that we could plant the seed of Christ. By the end of the week, he wanted to hear our testimonies. I had mine before evening fell.

It was Buddy's twenty-sixth birthday, and we were celebrating by having a barbecue in the afternoon. I didn't go to the cemetery after church like I usually do because I had to prepare for his party. Around five o'clock, I managed to slip away to take Mikey flowers. It was a beautiful April afternoon and very peaceful there. I had not yet prayed to God about my pastor's challenge. Matter of fact, I wasn't sure I felt like it. I knew I should, but I wrestled with the prayer. As I was taking the wilted flowers out of the vase, I grumbled to God that my soul was tired and I was going to take a break that week. I didn't feel like bringing any more broken hearts my way.

Walking over to the faucet to get some water, I noticed a white pickup parked across the way. I ignored it, reached the faucet, and began to rinse the grass off the angel that Rosy had left at the grave. Then I heard a voice calling out to me. I turned around and saw a young man in his early thirties standing about fifty feet from me.

"Excuse me," he said, "do you mind my asking who you are visiting?"

"No, not at all," I replied. "I'm visiting my son."

"Oh, I'm sorry to hear that. How old was he?"

"He was seventeen."

"How did he die?" he asked.

I shared my story, and when I was finished, I could tell that he wanted to continue talking.

"Who are you visiting?" I asked.

"My brother and my mother."

"Wow, both of them." I figured it was a car accident, and I was about to ask when he started talking again.

"I was only a year old when my brother died so I didn't really know him. He was ten years old. Got run over by a tractor. My mom started drinking and became an alcoholic," he said.

The man proceeded to tell me that his father tried to get his mom help, but nothing worked and she eventually died of cirrhosis of the liver. My heart began to ache for him. If his mother started drinking when he was a year old, then he never had the opportunity to know his mom either. He only knew the alcoholic mother. What a tragedy.

"You know, your mother may have clinically died from cirrhosis of the liver, but her primary diagnosis was a broken heart. It's a hard thing to go through. I hope you can have forgiveness in your heart for her."

"When did your son die?" he asked.

"Five years ago."

"You seem to be doing okay, how are you getting through it?" he quietly asked.

"Well, it's not easy. I miss my son terribly, and I mourn for him every single day, but I am getting through it because I believe what happened on Calvary. I believe that Jesus died on the cross for my sins and rose again in three days so that I may have eternal life. I believe in heaven above, and I know that I will see my son again. I'm getting through it because I have hope."

The man stood very still, raised his hand, and with his index finger, wiped his eye. Then without saying another word, he got into his truck and left. I'm not sure, but I think he was wiping away a tear.

Several months later, I had another encounter with a man while standing at that same faucet. He was sitting on the ground bent over a grave when he heard the water pouring into my watering can. He looked up and said, "Ahaa, water! I was just wondering how I was going to give my wife's roses a drink."

"Faucet's been here for the past five and a half years that I know of," I announced.

He got up off the ground, his mini rose plant in his hand, and came to the faucet. It was obvious that the man had been crying.

"I guess you think I must be nuts sitting here talking to my dead wife."

"Not at all. Maybe if I were on the outside of the fence looking in, I'd think you are a bit crazy, but I'm not. I'm on the same side of the fence with you. I understand your pain."

"My wife died over a year ago, and I'm still leaving her love letters. Is that insane or what?"

"You do what you have to do in order to heal. We all do." Pointing to a grave near his wife's, I said, "See that grave? It belongs to a young woman from Cambodia. Every so often her husband leaves a platter of fruit for her. It stays until it rots and then it's gone. Must be some kind of tradition or maybe she loved fruit." I paused for a moment. "The grave next to your wife belongs to Jose and—"

"Whoa, what are you? Some kind of graveyard groupie?" he interrupted.

I have been called a lot of things in my life, but this had to take the cake. Graveyard groupie? At first, I was stunned; and for a split second, I didn't know what to think. Then we both started laughing hysterically. When the laughter died down, the man looked at me, and with tears in his eyes he said that he has not laughed like that in a long time.

"You are a funny lady," he said. "I hope to see you again."

When I think about that man, I always smile, and it is a story that I love to share. It always makes people laugh. I love to make people laugh.

Most of the people I meet in Oak View Memorial Park, the cemetery where Mikey is buried, are just graveyard friends. Our paths have not crossed outside the cemetery. Not once have I ever seen any of them in the local stores. It seems that God has a different plan for me on the other side of the fence. I have the friends I've known for many years, and I have my church family. I also meet new people, many who are going through the same journey that I am. Mothers who are suffering the loss of a child seem to gravitate toward one another. We share a special bond because we understand each other's pain. God sets the stage and brings us together in the most unusual places, sometimes standing a long grocery line or outside in a parking lot.

My friend Robin, whose fifteen-year-old son died, was sent to me by my friend Deanna, whom I met at the crisis center just five months after Mikey died. Deanna's husband is a doctor who once treated me. You can imagine my surprise when I walked into the crisis center and saw him sitting there with his wife. I was stunned to see them there, and for the first time, I realized that death does not discriminate. I was to learn that their son died just one month before Mikey. Deanna and I became fast friends, and for years, we meet every few months for dinner. Same place, same time. She has a heart of gold and has helped me through a journey that I did not want to partake in.

Several years after her son passed away, Deanna became a grief counselor at the crisis center. Deanna was going on vacation and gave Robin my number in the event that she needed someone to talk to while she was away. Robin and I met and became friends. Several years later, Robin shared a graveyard story that touched the chambers of my heart.

It's not my story, but I want to share it with you because it is probably one of the most compassionate stories I have ever heard and I am sure it will touch your heart.

Robin was at Union Cemetery visiting her son. It was cold and getting late when she finally decided to go home. As she was leaving, she spotted her friend Allison whose son had just passed away. She got out of her car and went to her. She stood quietly with Allison for a while then told her that she needed to go home. "Allison," she said, "it's getting late and it's cold. You need to go home now."

"I'm not leaving Chad."

"You need to go home, it's not safe for you to be here alone."

"I'm not leaving," she cried.

Robin knew that Allison wasn't going anywhere so she took out her cell phone and called her husband. She told him that Allison was at the cemetery and wouldn't leave so she was staying there with her. Then she quietly told Allison to move over, crawled in Allison's sleeping bag, and spent the night with her. There, in the cold, dark cemetery, on top of Chad's grave lay two mothers with broken hearts, one comforting the other, and there is no doubt in my mind that God was right there in the middle, watching over them.

Deanna once told me that the cemetery is a community all in itself. That is such a true statement. In every cemetery, there are people with broken hearts reaching out to one another. Not just mothers mourning for their children. There are friends mourning for friends, children mourning for their parents, siblings mourning for siblings, and spouses mourning for their spouse. Everyone has suffered a loss.

For me, the loss of a child has to be the most horrific pain that the human soul will ever have to endure. I don't think there could be a greater loss than that of a child, however; I have come to understand that there are different levels of pain. When someone you love passes away, there is pain. Regardless of who passed away, it leaves a hole in your heart. You have reached a level of pain that you have never felt before and it hurts. It hurts so bad that it literally takes your breath away.

When I go to the cemetery and see new graves, it breaks my heart to see the pain on the faces of those that are left behind, especially an elder whose spouse has passed away. I don't know how it feels to lose a spouse. I can only imagine that it must feel like you have just lost a limb. Pain is pain regardless of the loss.

I don't go to the cemetery to mourn for Mikey anymore. I go there to honor my son by bringing him pretty flowers and spend quiet time with Jesus. I also go to the cemetery to shine the light of hope and share the Gospel of Christ to those that are in distress. There is no greater feeling witnessing the first signs of joy returning to the heart of someone who has finally overcome their grief. It is also a wonderful feeling when I get out of my car and someone hollers my name and with a smile on their face they come to me with open arms.

These are my graveyard friends.

Tapestry Of Our Life

Karen M. Kelly

Life is that of a tapestry, our joys and sorrows finely woven together and entwined with the trials and tribulations that the world has to offer us. The first stitch is sewn at birth. The final stitch at death.

God has a divine plan for each of us. He knows how our tapestry will be woven even before we are born. God knows the number of our days. Each single stitch represents one complete day on earth. He knows how many stitches will be sewn together before our tapestry is completed. No two tapestries will be alike. The patterns that are formed and the colors that are present are a symbol of our uniqueness, each beautiful in its own way.

The pattern of my life shows a remarkable change when the thread of the 16,816 stitch was woven into my tapestry. The once bright and vibrant colors are muted. Shades of gray are sewn, giving the illusion of fog. Splashes of red symbolizing the spilling of blood and a broken heart. The thread creates a black circle, which represents a valley that I have entered. There is a fine point of dim yellow in the center of the black. The yellow is my hope. As I walk through the valley, pale blue droplets are woven to represent my tears. The journey is long and tiresome, but as I continue my walk, the yellow grows brighter, illuminating the black.

The gray is no longer visible. The muted colors are bright once again. The fog has lifted. Moments of joy now gives rest to the sorrow that will always be present.

On November 20, 2001, the tapestry of my seventeen-and-a-half-year-old son's tapestry was completed. The final stitch sewn.

A legacy was born 6,333 stitches later.

At one o'clock on a Tuesday afternoon, bright colors of blue, white, and golden yellow were delicately woven, symbolizing that my precious son had ascended into heaven. At the sound of the last trumpet, the angels appeared and carried him through the gates of heaven, which are made of a single pearl. There he sees the face of Jesus who greeted him with open arms. A crown of eternal life was placed on his head, and all tears were wiped away. Mikey now walks streets paved in gold. He has a glorified body and a new heavenly name. Mikey is busy in heaven. What he is doing is not known to me. I can only imagine.

Epilogue

Before I left the hospital that fatal day, I was given a standard-size manila envelope. When I got home, I tossed it on the brick hearth in front of the fireplace. The contents frightened me. It smelled like a hospital.

There was a chill in the house so my husband kept the heat on and the fireplace burning to bring warmth. The chill remained. I couldn't get warm. I spent many hours in Mikey's room or lying on the carpet in front of the fire. I wanted to hibernate and not wake up until the nightmare was over. I wanted my Mikey back!

In my quiet moments, I spent time with God and tried to imagine all the glories of heaven. Visions of my son in the arms of Jesus gave me comfort. It didn't take away the pain. Just gave me enough comfort and peace to keep me sane. I was also sorting through the stories I was hearing about the day of the accident. So much sadness however, as strange as it sounds, very touching to hear how Joel and Mikey's tragedy impacted people far beyond our little community of Oakley. I was sorry that Joel also passed, but so very grateful that Mikey transitioned in heaven with his best buddy. They are still together!

It was also during this time that I remembered the helicopter I saw on the morning of the accident.

The office where I worked was located on the third floor of Salvio Pacheco Square at the Todos Santos Plaza in Concord. In order to use the restroom, we had to go to the lobby. Melchia and I returned from our morning walk at ten thirty. I was settled at my desk, for a while, then left to use the ladies' room. As I was walking along the balcony, I looked up and saw the medical helicopter and prayed. It was coming from the east and heading toward John Muir Hospital. My God, was I praying for my own son?

As time passed, my thoughts would wander back to that morning. I would go months without thinking about it, but it would sneak back into my mind and haunt me. Several years later, I called Reach Air Ambulance and talked to a very nice young man. Unfortunately, too much time had gone by and he was not working for them at the time of the accident. He did say that there was a possibility that they did fly over the area. It was a route they might have taken. The time that it would have taken to get from Oakley to John Muir was about eight minutes, give or take a few minutes, depending on the wind factors. I don't know why it was so important for me to know this information. I guess I was trying to piece it all together to achieve some type of closure. I was to learn that there will never be any closure. I can't wrap up all my love for Mikey in a tidy box and put it away. Seventeen years of his life are stored in my heart. Sometimes a memory is awakened while digging in the yard, little toy treasures lost through the years. These finds used to bring buckets of tears. Now they bring a smile. I've cleaned off a few and saved them, but most are reburied. It doesn't matter if it is Buddy's toy or Mikey's. I just like marking their existence in our yard.

I eventually opened the manila envelope that smelled like a hospital. It contained pamphlets and loose papers about the five stages of grief and the journey I would need to work through. I remember being glad that I didn't open the envelope and read any of the information when Mikey first passed. At that time, I didn't want anyone telling me how to process my grief.

By the time I opened the envelope, I was able to focus on what I was reading. One of the stages of grief is acceptance. It has taken me many, many years to finally accept Mikey's death. I could not have reached this stage without my faith in God. He gave me the strength to continue on, along with family and friends to help me through such a dark time.

I originally started writing about Mikey for myself. As I began to reminisce and capture our life on paper, I realized how therapeutic and healing it was. Reliving our moments together kept him close to me.

I hope to have my next manuscript completed and ready to be published by summer 2019.

Good Night, Mikey, I Love You Too is about all the crazy and wonderful things that was done to heal our souls and reach acceptance.

CPSIA information can be obtained
at www.ICGtesting.com
Printed in the USA
FSHW011056040119
54830FS